MATHS & ENGLISH FOR
PLUMBING

Graduated exercises and practice exam

Andrew Spencer and Gary Taylor

CENGAGE
Learning·

Australia • Brazil • Japan • Korea • Mexico • Singapore • Spain • United Kingdom • United States

Maths & English for Plumbing

Andrew Spencer and Gary Taylor

Publishing Director: Linden Harris

Publisher: Lucy Mills

Development Editor: Claire Napoli

Editorial Assistant: Lauren Darby

Production Editor: Alison Burt

Manufacturing Buyer: Eyvett Davis

Typesetter: Cambridge Publishing Management Limited

Cover design: HCT Creative

For product information and technology assistance, contact **emea.info@cengage.com**.

For permission to use material from this text or product, and for permission queries, email **emea.permissions@cengage.com**.

This work is adapted from *Pre Apprenticeship: Maths & Literacy Series* by Andrew Spencer published by Cengage Learning Australia Pty Limited © 2010.

British Library Cataloguing-in-Publication Data
A catalogue record for this book is available from the British Library.

ISBN: 978-1-4080-8310-9

Cengage Learning EMEA Cheriton House, North Way, Andover, Hampshire, SP10 5BE United Kingdom

Cengage Learning products are represented in Canada by Nelson Education Ltd.

For your lifelong learning solutions, visit **www.cengage.co.uk**

Purchase your next print book, e-book or e-chapter at **www.cengagebrain.com**

Printed in Greece by Bakis
1 2 3 4 5 6 7 8 9 10 – 15 14 13

Maths & English for Plumbing

Contents

Introduction

It has always been important to understand, from a teacher's perspective, the nature of the mathematical skills students need for their future, rather than teaching them textbook mathematics. This has been a guiding principle behind the development of the content in this workbook. To teach maths and English that is relevant to students seeking apprenticeships is the best that we can do, to give students an education in the field that they would like to work in.

The content in this resource is aimed at the level that is needed for a student to have the best possibility of improving their maths and English skills specifically for trades. Students can use this workbook to prepare for an Functional Skills assessment, or even to assist with basic Maths and English for their qualification. This resource has the potential to improve the students' understanding of basic maths concepts that can be applied to trades. These resources have been trialled, and they work.

Commonly used industry terms are introduced so that students have a basic understanding of terminology that they will encounter in the workplace environment. (Words that are in the glossary appear in **bold** the first time they are used.) Students who can complete this workbook and reach a higher outcome in all topics will have achieved the goal of this resource.

The content in this workbook is the first step towards bridging the gap between what has been learnt in previous years, and what needs to be remembered and re-learnt for use in exams and in the workplace. Students will significantly benefit from the consolidation of the basic maths and English concepts.

In many ways, it is a win–win situation, with students enjoying and studying relevant maths and English for work and training organizations and employers receiving students that have improved basic maths and English skills.

All that is needed is patience, hard work, a positive attitude, a belief in yourself that you can do it and a desire to achieve. The rest is up to you.

About the authors

Andrew Spencer has studied education within both Australia and overseas. He has a Bachelor of Education, as well as a Masters of Science in which he specialized in teacher education. Andrew has extensive experience in teaching secondary mathematics throughout New South Wales and South Australia for well over fifteen years. He has taught a range of subject areas, including Maths, English, Science, Classics, Physical Education and Technical Studies. His sense of the importance of practical mathematics has continued to develop with the range of subject areas he has taught in.

This workbook has been adapted by **Gary Taylor**. Gary is a plumbing curriculum leader at a large college in the North West of England. Gary has over thirty-five years' experience in the plumbing industry, of which twenty years were spent running his own successful plumbing company, installing central heating systems, bathrooms and servicing gas equipment.

Acknowledgements

Andrew Spencer:
  For Paula, Zach, Katelyn, Mum and Dad.
  Many thanks to Mal Aubrey (GTA) and all training organizations for their input.
  Thanks also to the De La Salle Brothers for their selfless support and ongoing work with all students.
  To Dr Pauline Carter for her unwavering support of all Maths teachers.
  This is for all students who value learning, who are willing to work hard and who have character . . .
  and are characters!

Gary Taylor:
  For my wife and best friend Carol for her support over the past thirty years, and to my daughters Rachael and
  Leanne for giving me some wonderful memories over the years.

The publisher would like to thank the many copyright holders who have kindly granted us permission to reproduce material throughout this text. Every effort has been made to contact all rights holders, but in the unlikely event that anything has been overlooked, please contact the publisher directly and we will happily make the necessary arrangements at the earliest opportunity.

ENGLISH

Unit 1: Spelling

Short-answer questions

Specific instructions to students

- This is an exercise to help you to identify and correct spelling errors.
- Read the following activity and answer accordingly.

Read the following passage and identify and correct the spelling errors.

A plumber needs to re-fit a bathroom. It needs a signifikant amount of work. The toilet needs a new cisctern, as well as a new **WC** pan. In addision, the sinc and the shouwer need to be replased. The cost of the new parts is a magor considerution. The managor wants the job completed by Saturduy. The aprentice replaces most of the parts on the toliet **cistern** first, and then moves on to secure the cistern to the wall currectly.

There are a numbar of screws that need replacing, along with several wushers. The showur skreen has a damiged hunge that will need to be removed and repared. The apprentise uses a skrewdriver to remove the six screws on the hinge. One is dufficult to remove, so he sprays the screw with lubricant and then uses a different screwdrivur to remove it. The boss indikates that he waunts the watur turned off before proceding. The old sink has suveral deep skratches in it and it therefor needs to be thrown out and replaced with a new one. It takes ovur eight hours to complete the job; however, everything turns out well and is finished by the time to pack up comes aroond.

Incorrect words:

_____

_____

_____

Correct words:

_____

_____

_____

Unit 2: Grammar and Punctuation

Short-answer questions

Specific instructions to students

- The following questions will help you to practise your grammar and punctuation.
- Read the following questions and answer accordingly.

Task 1 ⓛ

QUESTION 1

Which linking word or phrase could you use instead of 'Whereas'?

Answer:

_____

QUESTION 2

What does the linking word 'alternatively' mean?

Answer:

_____

QUESTION 3

What **punctuation** is missing from the following **sentences**?

A full range of services are available including inspection repair and testing of all makes of central heating boilers pumps controls and electrical faults. All at competitive rates.

Answer:

_____

QUESTION 4

What is wrong with the following text? Correct the following sentences.

Last week was a very busy week for harry. He had to travel from manchester to london to complete a bathroom installation. Because he had help from his apprentice joe, the job was finished on time.

Answer:

_____

_____

QUESTION 5

When you have completed a section of writing, what should you look for when checking through your work?

Answer:

_____

_____

QUESTION 6

What is wrong with the following text?

Why not visit our new luxury bathroom showroom set in the heart of rural Lancashire? Youre sure to receive a warm welcome, and be shown the latest models of luxury bathroom suites we have available. Our fully trained staff are on hand to cater for your every need. To find out more or book an appointment, call Andrew on 01435 778367.

Answer:

_____

_____

QUESTION 7

Can you identify the mistake in this job application letter?

Dear Madam

I wish to apply for the vacancy of sales adviser at your luxury bathroom showroom, as advertised in this week's Lancashire Globe.

I have just completed my Level 2 NVQ Diploma in Plumbing and Central Heating course at Dinsdale Park Colleage and am now looking for work in the Lancashire area.

I enclose a copy of my CV and look forward to hearing from you.

Yours faithfully

Luke Smith

Answer:

_____

QUESTION 8

Can you identify the mistakes in this advert?

> **Bathrooms to Go, West London**
>
> Bathrooms to go is located in West London and is your one stop shop for bathroom's and accessories. At bathrooms to go our highly trained staff will be on hand to insure your visit is one to remember and guide you round our luxury range of bathrooms and accessories. Please ring 0151 629 40276 to find out more about our special services.

Answer:

QUESTION 9

Add **commas** to the following text to make the sense clearer.

> Cleaning an oil spill is a very simple task when done correctly. An oil spillage can be very dangerous. Someone could easily slip on the oil or if there is a large amount it could also be a fire **hazard**. Spillages should be cleaned up as soon as they happen – a small amount of oil can easily be soaked up with an absorbent cloth. If a large oil spillage occurs you should soak it up with absorbent granules.
>
> Allow them to soak in for a few hours. When the oil has soaked in sweep the granules up and treat them as hazardous waste. They should be stored until you have a large amount and then be collected by a specialist waste company for correct disposal. If the floor still has a greasy feel use some diluted detergent and mop the floor then allow to dry.

Answer:

Task 2

Read the following paragraph and then add punctuation and capital letters where required.

water is the earths most valuable resource humans plants and animals cannot survive without it water originates from clouds where condensation forms water droplets that fall as rain into rivers and the sea the remainder soaks into the ground from where especially during summer evaporation takes place and the whole cycle begins again this is commonly known as the water cycle most of the water used in the north west of england comes from the lake district which is well known for its annual rainfall taking steps to save water is the responsibility of everyone

Answer:

Unit 3: Homophones

Short-answer questions

Specific instructions to students

- The following questions relate to words that sound the same, but are spelt differently and have different meanings. These words are known as **homophones**.
- Read the following questions carefully and answer accordingly.

QUESTION 1

The following sentences are about two apprentices that have decided to go on holiday together.

a   Check your knowledge of *there*, *their* and *they're* in the following sentences. Only one sentence is correct. Which one is it?

   (1) They're too many customers booked in on Friday, for the number of plumbers.

   (2) The manager realized that there holiday will be taken the same time as two others.

   (3) They're going on their holiday in the early hours of Friday morning.

   (4) There going to be short staffed on Friday, as their's two plumbers off sick.

   Answer:

   _____

b   Check your knowledge of *where*, *were* and *we're* in the following sentences. Only one sentence is correct. Which one is it?

   (1) When we get to our destination, we're not sure were we'll go first.

   (2) We're sure we'll be fine when we know where we're going.

   (3) If there's a delay, where sure that we're going to miss our connecting flight.

   (4) Once we find the hotel, were going to shower and change and go straight out.

   Answer:

   _____

c   Check your knowledge of *too*, *to* and *two* in the following sentences. Only one sentence is correct. Which one is it?

   (1) The two of us are going to go on holiday to New York too.

   (2) We want to go too Staten Island too.

   (3) We're concerned that there'll be two many people on the Metro in New York.

   (4) To get too Staten Island, the two of us will need to catch the ferry.

   Answer:

   _____

d   Check your knowledge of *buy*, *by* and *bye* in the following sentences. Only one sentence is correct. Which one is it?

   (1) We'll each have to bye a ticket to get to Staten Island by ferry.

   (2) By the way, we'll have to make sure that we buy plenty of souvenirs to take home.

   (3) Buy the time we get home, it will be a struggle to say bye to each other.

   (4) By all accounts, we'll have to bye some waterproofs for the ferry journey.

   Answer:

   _____

e Check your knowledge of *pause, paws* and *pours* in the following sentences. Only one sentence is correct. Which one is it?

(1) If it paws down with rain, we'll go to Central Park Zoo.

(2) If there's a pause in the rain, we'll go and see the polar bears.

(3) It doesn't matter if their pours get wet, as they'll be swimming in their pool anyway.

(4) Once it starts raining, though, it just paws and paws.

Answer:

_____

f Check your knowledge of *heal, he'll* and *heel* in the following sentences. Only one sentence is correct. Which one is it?

(1) While running in the rain, I slipped and fell on my knee and broke the heal of my shoe.

(2) My knee is really sore and bruised, so it will take a couple of days to heel.

(3) I'm so glad that Andrew is with me, as he'll have to lend me a bit of support.

(4) I couldn't find a cobbler, so I'll have to wait to get my heal fixed when I get home.

Answer

_____

QUESTION 2

Check your knowledge of *there, their* and *they're* in the following sentences. Read each sentence and write the correct word in the space provided, from the words provided below:

there   **their**   **they're**

a When they have finished this job, _____ going to have lunch.

b _____ was just enough pipe to finish the job.

c I wonder if I could move the **radiator** over _____?

d I have asked the customer to move all of _____ valuable items in the lounge.

e It's nearly 11.00 a.m. and _____ going to be here in a minute.

f There's a new tool range in stock; I've heard that _____ really good.

g I believe that the suppliers have got all of _____ new bathrooms in stock.

h I'll have to go to the suppliers again; I was only _____ last week.

i I must leave work on time to get to the suppliers before _____ closed.

QUESTION 3

Check your knowledge of *where, were* and *we're* in the following sentences. Read each sentence and write the correct word in the space provided, from the words provided below:

where   **were**   **we're**

a We always make sure the customer knows _____ we are with the work before leaving the job.

b _____ always sure to tidy the customers house before leaving a job.

c If the tools are damaged _____ not prepared to use them for health and safety reasons.

d When setting out equipment, we always have everything laid out _____ it is in easy reach of the plumber.

e When installing a radiator, _____ always checking to make sure it is level.

f We always make sure that any soldering work is carried out _____ there is a fire extinguisher.

g _____ always on time when attending a job.

h We always make sure the tools are locked safely in the van; there's nothing worse than if they _____ stolen.

i If we _____ not to offer any aftercare advice, as part of the installation service, we would be providing a disservice to the customer.

j _____ always happy when customers book in for another boiler service, as it shows that they _____ satisfied with the service they received.

QUESTION 4

The following chart relates to words that sound the same, but are spelt differently and have different meanings (**homophones**). Complete the chart, where applicable, providing clues for the word's meaning and/or a short sentence to put the word in the correct context.

Words	Clues for meaning	Short sentence
Hear	To listen to	
Here	In this spot	
Weak		I felt so weak this morning, I could hardly move.
Week	A period of 7 consecutive days	
Piece		I'll only have a small piece of chocolate cake, thank you.
Peace	Freedom from strife, arguments or war	
Cue		During the play, he spotted his cue to speak.
Queue	To form a line while waiting	
Allowed		
Aloud		You're not meant to speak aloud in a library.
Knew	The past tense of 'know'	
New		
Stationery	Writing materials such as pens, pencils, paper and envelopes	
Stationary		Locking the castors on a stool makes it stationary.
Whole	The complete sum, amount or quantity of anything	
Hole		I must have lost my money through the hole in my pocket.
Draught	A current of air, usually of a different temperature, entering an enclosed space	
Draft	A first sketch, or version, of writing, which could be subject to revision	
Draw		
Drawer	A lidless container that slides in and out of a chest or table	

Short-answer questions

Specific instructions to students

- These exercises will help you to understand what you read.
- Read the following activities and answer the questions that follow.

Comprehension Task 1

Read the following passage and answer the questions in sentence form.

Paul the foreman plumber had to be onsite early on Monday to work on a cold water service and supply pipe that had burst. He arrived at 6.45 a.m. and he began the task of identifying why the leak had occurred and what was needed to repair both pipes. One of his team, Steven, had to go to hospital the previous day as he had injured his shoulder lifting a heavy cast iron pipe into place. He was going to be off sick for a while, although Paul had several other plumbers he could call upon to repair the leaking pipes. The first to arrive was Geoff, the apprentice. Paul immediately showed Geoff the leaking cold water pipes and advised him what was needed to repair the 28 mm **MDPE** cold water **service pipe** and the leaking copper 15 mm cold water supply pipe. Both pipes would need replacing and Geoff understood the details of the task. While Paul was discussing the leaking pipes with Geoff, another plumber, Andrew, arrived to help. Andrew was a very experienced plumber and had been in the trade for over thirty years. Andrew knew immediately what was needed to repair both pipes. On further investigation it was found that the pipes had been damaged by a **JCB excavator** while digging the foundations for a new extension. There was extensive damage to both pipes and they needed to make sure that the water was turned off at the external stop valve before they could begin the task of repairing the damaged pipes. However, before Paul or Andrew could begin the task of repairing the 28 mm MDPE pipe, their first priority was to make sure that the area was safe and accessible to carry out the repair works needed.

Andrew returned to the company vehicle to get the necessary tools required for the repair job, while Paul made the working area safe and accessible. Meanwhile, Geoff was busy measuring the length of copper pipe that he needed to repair the cold water supply pipe. Geoff inspected the damage and precisely measured the amount of 15 mm copper pipe needed for the repair to the cold water supply pipe. The job was not difficult, but Geoff knew that at some stage he would need to solder the pipes. He went to the company vehicle, and brought back the **LPG** blow lamp, heat mat and, most important, the fire extinguisher. Geoff then set about the task of repairing the 15 mm supply pipe but was unsure of how to solder the copper pipe safely. He asked Paul's advice about the best way to solder the pipe and so Paul came over to give Geoff a hand and advise on the best way to solder the 15 mm copper pipe safely. Within two hours they had completed the job, leaving both Geoff and Paul free to assist Andrew in fixing the damaged cold water service MDPE pipe. It was in the middle of winter, and so both the sun and the afternoon quickly drew to a close and it was starting to get dark and cold. Paul, Andrew and Geoff completed most of the work by 4.30 p.m., knowing that they would need to return early next morning to complete the outstanding repair work.

QUESTION 1

Why did Paul have to be on site early?

Answer:

QUESTION 2

What was the first job that Paul needed to do?

Answer:

QUESTION 3

Who replaced the copper 15 mm supply pipe?

Answer:

QUESTION 4

Why did Geoff ask Paul for advice?

Answer:

QUESTION 5

How long was Paul's working day? State your answer in hours and minutes.

Answer:

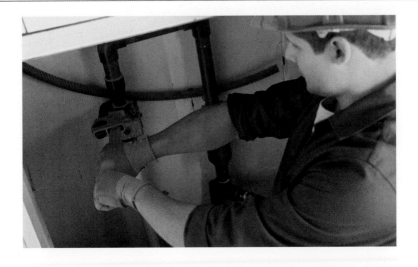

Comprehension Task 2

Read the following passage and answer the questions below.

Natural gas was formed some 200 million years ago, long before humans walked the planet! The formation of natural gas began with plants and small organisms dying and then being covered by mud, silt and lots of sand. Heat and pressure from the Earth's core turned the decaying plants and organisms into fossils and then eventually into petrol, oil and finally natural gas.

Natural gas, in its unadulterated form, has no colour and has no smell. The familiar 'gas' smell is added later in the collection process so that any leaks can be identified – gas is potentially explosive. Natural gas is mainly formed by methane, but is also present as a mixture of combustible **hydrocarbons**, namely ethane, propane, butane and pentane. Because natural gas is not synthetic, but rather naturally formed, we will have to find alternative sources of energy to replace natural gas when it finally runs out.

QUESTION 1
How long ago did natural gas start to form?

Answer:

QUESTION 2
What two things when covered in mud, silt and sand formed natural gas?

Answer:

QUESTION 3

What two characteristics inside the Earth helped to form natural gas?

Answer:

QUESTION 4

What are three components of natural gas?

Answer:

QUESTION 5

Of what is natural gas primarily formed?

Answer:

QUESTION 6

Natural gas is a combustible mixture of what?

Answer:

Questions

Specific instructions to students

- These exercises will help you to practise writing formal letters.
- Read the following information on formal letter writing and write your own letters following the instructions provided.

A **formal** letter is a method of communication that uses a professional tone and manner. There are many reasons for writing a formal letter. It could be to order supplies, to identify a mistake that was committed or to apologize for an error. A formal letter should be clear, concise and courteous as well as following a set structure. This should include:

1. The sender's address

2. Name, title and company name

3. Date (day, month and year)

4. Heading to indicate the reason for writing the letter

5. Greeting (Dear Mr/Mrs/Sir/Madam)

6. Introductory **paragraph**

7. Middle paragraphs containing the relevant information behind writing the letter

8. Closing paragraph describing what action you expect the recipient to take and a courteous closing sentence

9. A complimentary close ('Yours faithfully' if you do not know the recipient or 'Yours sincerely' if you know the recipient)

10. Room for a signature

Section A: Letter of complaint

You have recently purchased a new 18-volt cordless drill from a well known tool and accessory supplier. Having only used it once, you notice that the hammer action does not work and the trigger is faulty. When you returned to the place where you bought it, the sales adviser was very dismissive of your concerns and refused to help you. Using the appropriate language, write a letter of complaint to the company's head office, setting out:

- What you purchased

- What is wrong with it

- How you were treated by the sales adviser

- What you would like the company to do to resolve your complaint.

Answer:

Section B: Job application letter

> ## Trainee Plumbing and Central Heating Installer
>
> **Location: Oldham, Lancashire**
>
> **Salary: £14,000 – rising to £17,000 per annum on qualification**
>
> We are currently recruiting for a Plumbing and Central Heating Installer who has commitment, ambition and a real desire to learn about a full range of plumbing and heating systems. Reporting to the On-site Supervisor, the successful applicant will be part of a small team responsible for the repair, maintenance and installation of plumbing and heating systems.
>
> The successful applicant must have:
>
> - A quality focus, taking pride in excellent workmanship
> - Enthusiasm to work hard
> - The ability to work as part of a team.
>
> Please send your application to Mr Andrew Briars, Oldham Services, North Way, Oldham, Lancs.

You have seen the above advert in your local paper with a vacancy for a trainee. Write a letter of application, setting out why you would like the job and the skills that you have that make you suitable for the job. Continue writing your letter using the blank Notes pages at the back of this workbook if required. Also provide a CV and a personal statement to compliment your letter.

Answer:

Answer (continued):

Questions

Specific instructions to students

- These exercises will help you to practise writing skills that you will need to use when working in the plumbing industry.
- Complete the writing exercises following the instructions provided.

Section A: Writing emails

Write an email to your customer, Mr Andrew Richardson, reminding him that his central heating boiler is due for an annual service in 30 days' time.

Answer:

To:

Subject:

Section B: Completing a job card

Fill in all of the sections of this job card for a Worcester combination 24i boiler, serial number WS223367589, that has been booked in for an annual service. During the service some parts needed replacing including: **pressure relief valve**, seals on the **heat exchanger** and a **pressure switch** hose. The customer's details are: Mrs Charlesworth, 22 Halifax Road, Small Town, Lancashire SL5 4RF. The owner will only be available on her mobile during the day the work is carried out. Her mobile phone number is 07853 384869.

CUSTOMER NAME:	DATE:	TIME:

ADDRESS:

TEL. HOME:	TEL. WORK:
MAKE OF BOILER:	DATE OF NEXT SERVICE:
MODEL:	

SERIAL NO.:

WORK REQUIRED:

DETAILS OF EXTRA WORK CARRIED OUT:

PARTS USED:

BOILER SAFE TO USE?:

INVOICE DATE:	INVOICE NO.:

CUSTOMER SIGNATURE _____

Section C: Work carried out on a job card

When you write up a job card for the work that has been carried out on a customer's property, it is important to give as much detail as possible. Otherwise the customer may not be charged for all of your work and you in turn could be paid less money.

QUESTION 1

You have been called out to repair a leaking cold water pipe under a kitchen sink. You find that 100 mm of 15 mm copper pipe and a washing machine tap need replacing. Give a full write-up of the work carried out.

Answer:

QUESTION 2

Give a full write up of the necessary work needed to replace a short piece of lead that is found on a hot water pipe in a bathroom.

Answer:

QUESTION 3

A customer has asked you to investigate a toilet that is overflowing. You notice that the ball valve arm has broken off. Give a full write-up of the necessary work needed to replace the ball valve.

Answer:

QUESTION 4

A customer has complained that her radiators are not getting hot. On investigation you find that the central heating pump has stopped working. Give a full write-up of work needed to replace the pump.

Answer:

Section D: Quotations and estimates

An **estimate** is not a fixed total price and can be amended as work progresses. A quotation is a fixed price and cannot be changed once given. Most plumbers opt to give estimates for reasons of flexibility. Estimates should include:

- Cost of labour

- Cost of materials

- Details of work to be carried out

- Estimated duration of time to complete the work

- Any special requirements needed to complete the work

- Any health and safety issues

- Full total cost for completed work.

A customer has requested an estimate to replace a bathroom suite. Using the information given above, provide a full detailed estimate of necessary work and cost to replace the bathroom suite. You can research cost details by going online or using suppliers' catalogues. Complete the form on the following page.

Answer:

PLUMBING ESTIMATE		
	Customer	
	Address	
	Phone	

Description of work to be done

Materials

Item	Qty	Price	Amount
		Total	

Labour

Hours	Rate	Amount
	Total	

Acceptance of estimate

Signature	Date

Total estimate

Total materials	
Total labour	
Subtotal	
VAT	

Section E: Completing a service invoice

Complete this blank invoice for the installation of a new bathroom suite and include all works completed. Give the customer a 10% discount and charge VAT at the current rate.

Answer:

INVOICE

DATE:

INVOICE:

CUSTOMER ID:

BILL TO:

DESCRIPTION	AMOUNT
Description of materials used	
SUBTOTAL	
Description of completed works	

SUBTOTAL

VAT RATE   %

DISCOUNT

OTHER

TOTAL DUE

OTHER COMMENTS

1. Total payment due in ten days

2. Please include the invoice number on your cheque

Make all cheques payable to

If you have any questions about this invoice, please contact

Thank You For Your Business!

Section F: Completing a risk assessment form

Fill in all the sections of this **risk assessment** for removing a washbasin and installing a new one in a college. The job consists of going into a home and looking for potential risks, making a materials list, taking out the old washbasin, putting in position the new one, piping up the washbasin, and leaving the area clean and tidy. Identify all potential hazards (including COSHH and PUWER), evaluate the risks (low/medium/high), describe all existing control measures and identify any further measures required.

Answer:

RISK ASSESSMENT			NO.
ASSESSED BY:			
AUTHORIZED BY:			
WORK ACTIVITY:			
TASK/HAZARD	RISK RATING	CONTROL MEASURES REQUIRED	ADDITIONAL REQUIREMENTS

IDENTIFY ALL NECESSARY PPE. TICK (✔) EACH THAT APPLIES.

EYE/FACE	HAND/ARM	FEET/LEGS	OTHERS (SPECIFY)
BODY (CLOTHING)	HEARING	RESPIRATORY	

PERSONS AT RISK: IDENTIFY ALL THOSE WHO MAY BE AT RISK. TICK (✔) EACH THAT APPLIES.

ACADEMIC STAFF	TECHNICAL STAFF	STUDENTS
MAINTENANCE STAFF	OFFICE STAFF	CLEANING STAFF
CONTRACTORS	VISITORS	OTHERS (SPECIFY)

LIST ALL THE EQUIPMENT, MATERIALS, TOOLS THAT YOU WILL USE IN THIS JOB

Section A: Comparing different types of text

Short-answer questions

Specific instructions to students

- This is an exercise to help you to identify different types of text.
- Read the following activity and answer accordingly.

Read each of the following paragraphs, state the purpose of each type of text, explain whether the text is formal or **informal** and why it is appropriate in this context.

Text A – Dave, can you pick up the radiator from the suppliers and go to the customer's property and install the radiator in the kitchen. Thanx Raj

Purpose of text:

_____

_____

Formal/informal:

_____

Why the text is appropriate:

_____

_____

_____

Text B – Place a small amount of silicon onto the shower door before pressing the rubber seal into the bottom groove. Once the rubber seal is in place, slide the shower door into position and secure to the tiled wall (see fig 008).

Purpose of text:

_____

_____

Formal/informal:

_____

Why the text is appropriate:

_____

_____

Text C – Please be advised that if this amount of money has not been paid in full, within 30 days of this notice, we will take legal proceedings to recover all of your outstanding debt.

Purpose of text:

_____

_____

Formal/informal:

_____

Why the text is appropriate:

_____

_____

Text D – Work carried out:

- Annual boiler service
- Checked CO/CO_2 levels
- Carried out gas safety check

Purpose of text:

_____

_____

Formal/informal:

_____

Why the text is appropriate:

_____

_____

_____

_____

Section B: Factual and subjective text

Short-answer questions

Specific instructions to students

- This is an exercise to help you to identify factual and subjective text.
- Read the following activity and answer the questions accordingly.

Text can either be factual or subjective.

If a piece of text is factual, it is based on real evidence and records of events which is not biased by the writer's opinion.

If a piece of text is subjective, it contains an individual's personal perspective, feelings or opinions which might differ from another individual's view of the same subject.

Which of the following is fact and which is opinion?

QUESTION 1

This type of radiator is the best that I have ever seen.

QUESTION 2

The government wants to reduce carbon emissions in the UK by 80% by the year 2050.

QUESTION 3

Combi boilers are the best type of boiler you can buy.

QUESTION 4

Paul is the best plumber that I have ever seen.

QUESTION 5

Employers and employees are responsible for health and safety while at work.

QUESTION 6

You must wear the appropriate **PPE** when you are working on a construction site.

QUESTION 7

The letters **CHP** stand for **combined heat and power**.

QUESTION 8

Baxi make the best boilers in the UK.

QUESTION 9

Makita make good quality tools.

QUESTION 10

Snap-on make tools for the plumbing trade.

QUESTION 11

Chrome spanners not only look good, they feel sturdy when you use them.

QUESTION 12

Only **SEDBUK** A-rated boilers can be installed in properties.

Section C: Appropriate tone and language

Short-answer questions

Specific instructions to students

- This is an exercise to help you to understand the appropriate tone and language to use in text.
- Read the following activity and answer the question accordingly.

Rewrite the below paragraph to make it more appropriate for its audience. Think specifically about the language, tone and purpose of the text.

For the manager of Top Plumbing Ltd

Your plumber did a bad job of fixing my boiler. The boiler is still noisy and your plumber was rude. He told me that I was imagining the noise and there was nothing wrong with the boiler. What your plumber did was wrong and he was bang out of order. I will be coming back into your service department on Friday and you will be giving me my money back.

From
Thomas Smith

Answer:

It is important to show your workings out to indicate how you calculated your answer. Use this workbook to practise the questions and record your answers. Use the blank Notes pages at the back of this book to record your workings out.

Unit 8: General Mathematics

Short-answer questions

Specific instructions to students

- This unit will help you to improve your general mathematical skills.
- Read the following questions and answer all of them in the spaces provided.
- You need to show all working, you can use the blank Notes pages at the back of this book.

QUESTION 1

Write the following in descending order:

0.4   0.04   4.1   40.0   400.00   4.0

Answer:

_____

QUESTION 2

Write the decimal number that is between:

a   0.2 and 0.4

Answer:

_____

b   1.8 and 1.9

Answer:

_____

c   12.4 and 12.6

Answer:

_____

d   28.3 and 28.4

Answer:

_____

e   101.5 and 101.7

Answer:

_____

QUESTION 3

Convert the following units:

a   12 kg to grams

Answer:

_____

b   120 cm to metres

Answer:

_____

c   1140 ml to litres

Answer:

_____

d   1650 g to kilograms

Answer:

_____

e   13 m to centimetres

Answer:

_____

f   4.5 l to millilitres

Answer:

_____

QUESTION 4

What unit of measurement would you use to measure:

a   A length of copper pipe?

Answer:

_____

b   The temperature of water?

Answer:

_____

c   The amount of central heating **inhibitor** in a bottle?

Answer:

_____

d   The weight of a combination boiler?

Answer:

_____

e   The flow rate of water?

Answer:

_____

f   The amount of silicon sealant?

Answer:

_____

g   The cost of a 3 m length of pipe?

Answer:

_____

QUESTION 5

Estimate the following by approximation:

a $1288 \times 20 =$

Answer:

_____

b $201 \times 20 =$

Answer:

_____

c $497 \times 12.2 =$

Answer:

_____

d $1008 \times 10.3 =$

Answer:

_____

e $399 \times 22 =$

Answer:

_____

f $201 - 19 =$

Answer:

_____

g $502 - 61 =$

Answer:

_____

h $1003 - 49 =$

Answer:

_____

i $10\,001 - 199 =$

Answer:

_____

j $99.99 - 39.8 =$

Answer:

_____

QUESTION 6

What do the following add up to?

a   £4, £4.99 and £144.95

Answer:

_____

b   8.75, 6.9 and 12.55

Answer:

_____

c   65 ml, 18 ml and 209 ml

Answer:

_____

d   21.3 g, 119 g and 884.65 g

Answer:

QUESTION 7

Subtract the following:

a   2338 from 7117

Answer:

---

b   1786 from 3112

Answer:

---

c   5979 from 8014

Answer:

---

d   11 989 from 26 221

Answer:

---

e   108 767 from 231 111

Answer:

QUESTION 8

Use division to solve the following:

a $2177 \div 7 =$

Answer:

---

b $4484 \div 4 =$

Answer:

---

c $63.9 \div 0.3 =$

Answer:

---

d $121.63 \div 1.2 =$

Answer:

---

e $466.88 \div 0.8 =$

Answer:

QUESTION 9

Write an example of the following and give an example of where it may be found in the plumbing industry.

a   **percentages**

Answer:

---

b   **decimals**

Answer:

---

c   **fractions**

Answer:

---

d   **mixed numbers**

Answer:

---

e   ratios

Answer:

---

f   angles

Answer:

QUESTION 10

Convert the following units:

a   4 to kilograms

Answer:

_____

b   1880 kg to tonnes

Answer:

_____

QUESTION 11

Round off the following numbers to two (2) decimal places:

a   12.346

Answer:

_____

b   2.251

Answer:

_____

c   123.897

Answer:

_____

d   688.882

Answer:

_____

e   1209.741

Answer:

_____

The following information is provided for Question 12.

To solve using BODMAS, in order from left to right, solve the Brackets first, then Order ('to the power of'), then Division, then Multiplication, then Addition and lastly Subtraction. The following example has been done for your reference.

QUESTION 12

Using BODMAS, solve:

a $(6 \times 9) \times 5 + 7 - 2 =$

Answer:

_____

b $(9 \times 8) \times (4 + 6) - 1 =$

Answer:

_____

c $3 \times 5 \times (7 + 11) - 8 =$

Answer:

_____

d $6 + (9 + 5 \times 8) \div 7 =$

Answer:

_____

e $(9 - 7) + 6 \times (3 + 9) \times 2^2 =$

Answer:

_____

f $2 \times (4 + 5^2) - (8 - 4) =$

Answer:

_____

Section A: Addition

Short-answer questions

Specific instructions to students

- This section will help you to improve your addition skills for basic operations.
- Read the following questions and answer all of them in the spaces provided.
- You need to show all working, you can use the blank Notes pages at the back of this book.

QUESTION 1

To replace a **soil pipe**, a plumber uses 2 m, 1 m, 3 m, 5 m and 7 m of pipe. How much pipe has been used in total?

Answer:

QUESTION 2

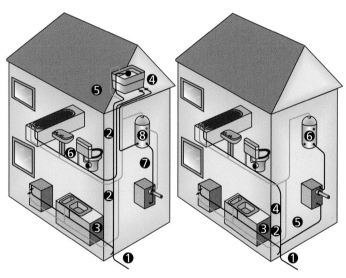

Indirect water system
1. service pipe from water company
2. rising main
3. drinking water from rising main
4. cold water storage tank
5. overflow pipe
6. cold feed pipe to bathroom
7. cold feed pipe to boiler
8. hot water cylinder

Direct water system
1. service pipe from water company
2. rising main
3. drinking water to kitchen
4. drinking water to bathroom
5. cold feed pipe to boiler
6. hot water cylinder

To re-plumb a bathroom, including a toilet and shower, a plumber uses 2.5 m, 1.8 m, 3.3 m and 5.2 m of copper pipe. How much pipe has been used in total?

Answer:

QUESTION 3

Armin the plumber is checking his stock of copper fittings and finds he has 46 15 mm **elbows**, 26 15 mm tees, 46 22 mm couplings and 18 22 mm elbows. How many copper fittings does Armin have in total?

Answer:

QUESTION 4

Susan the gas engineer is adding up her weekly mileage. Susan finds that she has driven 60 miles, 56 miles, 77 miles, 46 miles, 120 miles and 66 miles over a 6-day week. How far in total has Susan driven that week?

Answer:

QUESTION 5

An apprentice plumber uses the following amounts of diesel over a month:

Week 1: 35.5 l

Week 2: 42.9 l

Week 3: 86.9 l

Week 4: 66.2 l

a How many litres have been used in total?

Answer:

_____

b If diesel costs £1.95 per litre, how much would fuel have cost for the month?

Answer:

_____

QUESTION 6

Raj the apprentice plumber buys 4 waste pipe elbows for £16.99, 2 waste pipe tees for £12.60 and a length of 38 mm waste pipe for £7.80. How much has Raj spent altogether?

Answer:

_____

QUESTION 7

The following items are used on 3 plumbing jobs: 26 cross head screws, 52 metal washers and 48 rawl plugs. How many items have been used in total on the 3 plumbing jobs?

Answer:

_____

QUESTION 8

Some plastic fittings are bought for £125.80, a toilet for £166.99 and a new tap fitting for £88.50. How much has been spent?

Answer:

_____

QUESTION 9

An apprentice travels 36.8 miles, 98.7 miles, 77.2 miles and 104.3 miles over four days. How far has the apprentice travelled in total?

Answer:

_____

QUESTION 10

To complete some plumbing work on an industrial unit, 178 bolts, 188 nuts and 93 washers are used. How many parts are used?

Answer:

_____

Section B: Subtraction

Short-answer questions

Specific instructions to students

- This section will help you to improve your subtraction skills for basic operations.
- Read the following questions and answer all of them in the spaces provided.
- You need to show all working, you can use the blank Notes pages at the back of this book.

QUESTION 1

A vehicle is filled with petrol to its limit of 52 l. If the driver uses 22 l on one trip, 17 l on the second trip and 11 l on the third trip, how much is left in the tank?

Answer:

_____

QUESTION 2

If one plumber travels 362 miles and another plumber travels 169 miles, how much further has the first plumber travelled than the second?

Answer:

_____

QUESTION 3

Joe, the apprentice plumber, uses 39 rawl plugs from a box that originally contained 200 rawl plugs. How many rawl plugs are left in the box?

Answer:

QUESTION 4

A plumber uses the following amounts of drain cleaner for 3 jobs:

Job 1: 5.5 l

Job 2: 3.8 l

Job 3: 6.9 l

How much drain cleaner is now left in a drum that originally contained 20 l of drain cleaner?

Answer:

QUESTION 5

During one month, a plumber replaces 74 tap washers on several different jobs. If there were a total of 250 washers to begin with, how many tap washers are now left?

Answer:

QUESTION 6

A plumber's work van has a mileage reading of 78 769 miles before the start of a year. At the end of the year it reads 84 231 miles. What distance has the plumber travelled during the year?

Answer:

QUESTION 7

A plumber uses the following amounts of the same 110 mm soil pipe on 3 separate jobs: 8.7 m, 6.9 m and 15.3 m. If there were 50 m of pipe to begin with, how much is now left?

Answer:

QUESTION 8

Two central heating boilers are fuelled by LPG (liquid petroleum gas). Boiler A uses 243.8 l of LPG and boiler B uses 147.9 l of LPG. How much more does boiler A use than boiler B?

Answer:

QUESTION 9

Dave the plumber repairs a customer's central heating boiler at a cost of £224.65. Dave then gives the customer a 10% discount which is rounded off to £25.00. How much in total does the customer have to pay for the repair to the boiler?

Answer:

QUESTION 10

Over a year, an apprentice drives 12 316 miles in the company van. Of this, 5787 miles is for her own personal use. What distance did she travel for work purposes?

Answer:

Section C: Multiplication

Short-answer questions

Specific instructions to students

- This section will help you to improve your multiplication skills for basic operations.
- Read the following questions and answer all of them in the spaces provided.
- You need to show all working, you can use the blank Notes pages at the back of this book

QUESTION 1

If a car travels at 60 mph (miles per hour), how far will it travel in 4 hours?

Answer:

QUESTION 2

If a car travels at 70 mph, how far will it travel in 7 hours?

Answer:

QUESTION 3

A plumber uses 15 l of fuel for one trip. How much fuel will he use if he needs to complete the same trip 26 more times?

Answer:

QUESTION 4

An apprentice plumber uses 12 nuts, 14 washers and 8 bolts to assemble 1 shower enclosure. How many nuts, washers and bolts would be used if the plumber installed another 144 shower enclosures?

Answer:

QUESTION 5

A plumber uses 4 rawl bolts to secure one radiator to a masonry wall. How many rawl bolts would be needed to secure 12 radiators to a masonry wall?

Answer:

QUESTION 6

A work vehicle uses 9 l of petrol for every 100 miles travelled. How much petrol would be used for 450 miles?

Answer:

QUESTION 7

If a plumber used 73 tap washers on average per month, how many would he use over a year? (Note that there are 12 months in a year.)

Answer:

QUESTION 8

If a plumber uses 3 m of copper pipe each day over 28 days, how much pipe has she used in total?

Answer:

QUESTION 9

If a car travels at 65 mph for 5 hours, how far has it travelled?

Answer:

QUESTION 10

To complete a job on a building, 5 m of pipe with a 75 mm **diameter** is used on one section of the building, 2 m of pipe with a 50 mm diameter is used on another section, and 8 m of pipe with a 25 mm diameter is used on the last section. How much of each pipe would be used for 19 similar jobs?

Answer:

_____

_____

_____

_____

Section D: Division

Short-answer questions

Specific instructions to students

- This section will help you to improve your division skills for basic operations.
- Read the following questions and answer all of them in the spaces provided.
- You need to show all working, you can use the blank Notes pages at the back of this book.

QUESTION 1

A plumber has a 24 m length of 25 mm MDPE pipe. How many jobs can be completed if each standard job requires 3 m of pipe?

Answer:

_____

QUESTION 2

If a plumber earns £1125 (gross) for working a 5-day week, how much does the plumber earn per day?

Answer:

_____

QUESTION 3

A manager of a major plumbing company buys 14 000 l of fuel in bulk. Each of the fuel drums contains 180 l.

a How many drums are completely filled?

Answer:

_____

b Is any fuel left over?

Answer:

_____

QUESTION 4

An apprentice covers 78 miles in a 5-day week. On average, how many miles per day has he travelled?

Answer:

_____

QUESTION 5

The total weight of a 4WD work vehicle is 1488 kg. How much load, in kilograms, is on each wheel?

Answer:

_____

QUESTION 6

A plumber covers 925 miles over 27 days. How many miles has she covered, on average, per day?

Answer:

_____

QUESTION 7

During a yearly stocktake, a storeperson at a plumbing company counts 648 washers. There are 110 washers in each box.

a How many boxes are there?

Answer:

_____

b Are any washers left over?

Answer:

_____

QUESTION 8

A plumber orders 40 m of PVC pipe with a 110 mm diameter. If it is cut into 8 m lengths, how many lengths are there in total?

Answer:

_____

QUESTION 9

A van delivers 460 m of **PVC** pipe with a 42 mm diameter to a plumbing company. The piping will be used for 4 separate jobs, and the amount of piping for each job will be the same. How much piping will be allocated for each job?

Answer:

_____

QUESTION 10

A plumber travels over 890 miles over 28 days. How many miles has he travelled, on average, each day?

Answer:

_____

Unit 10: Decimals

Section A: Addition

Short-answer questions

Specific instructions to students

- This section will help you to improve your addition skills when working with decimals.
- Read the following questions and answer all of them in the spaces provided.
- You need to show all working, you can use the blank Notes pages at the back of this book.

QUESTION 1

A plumber buys a set of 4 tyres for a work vehicle, which comes to a total of £416.88. She then remembers that she needs a spare tyre, which costs another £45.50. What is the total cost of the 5 tyres?

Answer:

QUESTION 2

A plumber buys a circular saw for £39.95, a jigsaw for £29.95, several boxes of screws for a total of £44.55 and a new set of screwdrivers for £19.45. How much has been spent?

Answer:

QUESTION 3

Two lengths of 50 mm pipe measure 10.25 m and 8.48 m. What is the total length?

Answer:

QUESTION 4

A plumber buys the following: a washing machine hose for £8.99, a washing machine tap for £6.50, a tub of flux for £12.30 and a pipe freezing kit for £65.90. What is the total cost?

Answer:

QUESTION 5

If an apprentice plumber travels 65.8 miles, 36.5 miles, 22.7 miles and 89.9 miles over a week, how far has he travelled in total?

Answer:

QUESTION 6

What is the total length of a screwdriver with a handle of 15.5 cm and an end of 7.8 cm?

Answer:

QUESTION 7

A pipe has a diameter of 54.2 mm. Another pipe has a diameter of 75.9 mm. What is the overall combined diameter of both pipes when added together?

Answer:

QUESTION 8

A plumber completes 3 jobs. The following bills are charged for each job: £450.80 for the first job, £1130.65 for the second job and £660.45 for the third job. How much has been charged in total for all 3 jobs?

Answer:

QUESTION 9

A length of rainwater pipe measures 7.5 m. Another length of the same pipe measures 9.8 m. What is the total length of both rainwater pipes?

Answer:

QUESTION 10

Four central heating boiler **flue pipes** each have different diameters: 50.5 mm, 75.5 mm, 50.8 mm and 75.3 mm. What is the total of the combined diameters?

Answer:

Section B: Subtraction

Short-answer questions

Specific instructions to students

- This section will help you to improve your subtraction skills when working with decimals.
- Read the following questions and answer all of them in the spaces provided.
- You need to show all working, you can use the blank Notes pages at the back of this book.

QUESTION 1

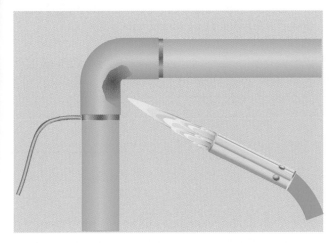

A length of 10 m copper pipe has several lengths cut from it. The lengths that were cut measured 3.8 m and 4.9 m.

a How much has been cut off?

Answer:

b How much is left?

Answer:

QUESTION 2

If a 4 m length of 75 mm PVC waste pipe has 22.5 cm cut from it, what length now remains?

Answer:

QUESTION 3

A plumber completes a job that costs £789.20 and then gives a discount of £75.50. How much is the final cost of the job?

Answer:

QUESTION 4

An apprentice works 38 hours and earns £245.60. She spends £48.85 on food, petrol and union fees; how much is left out of her wage?

Answer:

QUESTION 5

A connecting hot water pipe is 65.60 cm in length. A length of 8.95 cm is cut off. What amount remains?

Answer:

QUESTION 6

If one length of plastic soil pipe has a diameter of 95.5 mm and another has a diameter of 88.5 mm, what is the difference between the two?

Answer:

QUESTION 7

Paul the apprentice gas fitter decides to buy a new pipe slice. One is priced at £9.99 and another priced at £15.60. What is the cost difference between the two pipe slices?

Answer:

QUESTION 8

A plumber uses a 4 l container of wall tile adhesive for 3 different jobs: 285 ml for job 1, 560 ml for job 2, and 1300 ml on job 3. How much tile adhesive is left?

Answer:

QUESTION 9

An apprentice has a 4 m length of 25 mm MDPE water pipe. If 35 cm is cut off, then 76 cm and a further 44 cm, how much is left?

Answer:

QUESTION 10

Caroline has to connect a cold water supply to a new toilet. She has a 6 m length of pipe and cuts off 257 cm to connect the toilet. How much pipe is left over?

Answer:

Section C: Multiplication

Short-answer questions

Specific instructions to students

- This section will help you to improve your multiplication skills when working with decimals.
- Read the following questions and answer all of them in the spaces provided.
- You need to show all working, you can use the blank Notes pages at the back of this book.

QUESTION 1

If a tap costs £19.95 and a plumber needs 5 taps, how much will the total cost be?

Answer:

QUESTION 2

If a central heating engineer uses 16 l of central heating cleanser and each litre costs £10.50, what would the total cost be for 16 l?

Answer:

QUESTION 3

The following plumbing components are replaced in a home: 6 washers at a cost of £0.50 each and 8 spring washers at £0.99 each. What is the total cost?

Answer:

_____

QUESTION 4

If a plumber uses 6 packets of mirror screws that cost £8.65 each, how much does he pay?

Answer:

_____

QUESTION 5

An apprentice plumber purchases 12 packets of screws that cost £9.95 each from a hardware store. What is the total cost of the screws?

Answer:

_____

QUESTION 6

An apprentice earns £13.50 per hour. If the apprentice works a 45-hour week, how much will she earn?

Answer:

_____

QUESTION 7

A plumbing workshop owner buys a roll of 15 mm plastic cold water pipe for £2.55 per metre. If 25 m are purchased, how much is the total cost?

Answer:

_____

QUESTION 8

A plumber's work van has a 52 l tank. If petrol costs £1.55 per litre, how much would the total cost be for 52 l?

Answer:

_____

QUESTION 9

The owner of a large plumbing company purchases 3400 m of plastic guttering for £1.15 per meter. What is the total cost of the guttering?

Answer:

_____

QUESTION 10

A plumber earns £280.65 per day. If he works 5 days per week, how much will he have earned in one week?

Answer:

_____

Section D: Division

Short-answer questions

Specific instructions to students

- This section will help you to improve your division skills when working with decimals.
- Read the following questions and answer all of them in the spaces provided.
- You need to show all working, you can use the blank Notes pages at the back of this book.

QUESTION 1

A plumber has 28.5 l of drain cleaner that is needed for 6 separate jobs. How much needs to be allocated equally for each job?

Answer:

QUESTION 2

A plumber earns £990.60 for 5 days' work. How much does she earn per day?

Answer:

QUESTION 3

The bill for work on a vanity unit comes to £302.70. If the plumber splits the total evenly between himself and his apprentice, how much does each get?

Answer:

QUESTION 4

A master plumber completes a job on a bathroom. If the cost of labour is £280 and it takes 8 hours to complete the job, how much is the hourly rate?

Answer:

QUESTION 5

Stewart is delivering plumbing materials to his customers. Stewart covers 840 miles in 5 days. How far, on average, has he travelled per day?

Answer:

QUESTION 6

Mark the plumber drives 889.95 miles over 9 days. How far has he travelled per day?

Answer:

QUESTION 7

A car uses 72 l of diesel to travel 575.8 miles. How far can the car travel per litre?

Answer:

QUESTION 8

A plumbing workshop buys 360 kitchen tap sets, in bulk, at a total cost of £3200. How much is the cost of one tap set?

Answer:

QUESTION 9

It costs £90.95 to fill a 52 l fuel tank in the company's van. How much is the cost per litre?

Answer:

QUESTION 10

A 50 m roll of MDPE pipe costs £83.60. How much does it cost per metre?

Answer:

Unit 11: Fractions

Section A: Addition

Short-answer questions

Specific instructions to students

- This section is designed to help you to improve your addition skills when working with fractions.
- Read the following questions and answer all of them in the spaces provided.
- You need to show all working, you can use the blank Notes pages at the back of this book.

QUESTION 1

$\frac{1}{2} + \frac{4}{5} =$

Answer:

_____

QUESTION 2

$2\frac{2}{4} + 1\frac{2}{3} =$

Answer:

_____

QUESTION 3

A plumber pours $\frac{1}{3}$ of a bottle of pipe glue into a container. He then adds $\frac{1}{4}$ of another bottle into the same container. How much glue is in the container now in total? Express your answer as a fraction.

Answer:

_____

QUESTION 4

A bucket $\frac{1}{3}$ full of water is used to test the fall of a gutter. Another bucket is $\frac{1}{2}$ full. How much water is there in total? Express your answer as a fraction.

Answer:

_____

QUESTION 5

A plumber has $1\frac{2}{3}$ tubes of waterproof silicon. Another $1\frac{1}{4}$ tubes of the same silicon are also in the plumber's van. How much waterproof silicon is there in total? Express your answer as a fraction.

Answer:

_____

Section B: Subtraction

Short-answer questions

Specific instructions to students

- This section is designed to help you to improve your subtraction skills when working with fractions.
- Read the following questions and answer all of them in the spaces provided.
- You need to show all working, you can use the blank Notes pages at the back of this book.

QUESTION 1

$\frac{2}{3} - \frac{1}{4} =$

Answer:

_____

QUESTION 2

$2\frac{2}{3} - 1\frac{1}{4} =$

Answer:

_____

QUESTION 3

A plumber uses $\frac{2}{3}$ of a tube of sealant on a burst pipe. If a further $\frac{1}{2}$ of a tube is needed to complete the job, how much sealant is left in the tube? Express your answer as a fraction.

Answer:

_____

QUESTION 4

An apprentice has 3 bottles of drain cleaner. If $1\frac{2}{3}$ bottles of drain cleaner are used to clean a toilet, how much is left? Express your answer as a fraction.

Answer:

_____

QUESTION 5

A plumber has $2\frac{3}{4}$ tubes of silicon, and $1\frac{1}{2}$ tubes are used to seal an area in a shower. How much silicon is left in total? Express your answer as a fraction.

Answer:

_____

Section C: Multiplication

QUESTION 1

A plumber cuts 2 lengths of 75 mm downpipe, each measuring $18\frac{1}{2}$ cm. What is the total length cut? Express your answer as a fraction.

Answer:

QUESTION 2

A shower requires 4 lengths of $10\frac{1}{2}$ cm tile trim to complete the job. How much tile trim is needed in total? Express your answer as a fraction

Answer:

QUESTION 3

$\frac{2}{4} \times \frac{2}{3} =$

Answer:

QUESTION 4

$2\frac{2}{3} \times 1\frac{1}{2} =$

Answer:

QUESTION 5

A building needs $3\frac{1}{2}$ lengths of 50 mm plastic waste pipe that each measure $15\frac{1}{2}$ cm. How much waste pipe is needed in total? Express your answer as a fraction.

Answer:

Section D: Division

QUESTION 1

An apprentice has a length of 25 mm pipe that measures $26\frac{1}{2}$ cm. The apprentice needs to cut $2\frac{1}{2}$ equal lengths of the pipe. How long is each piece? Express your answer as a fraction.

Answer:

QUESTION 2

$2\frac{3}{4} \div 1\frac{1}{3} =$

Answer:

QUESTION 3

$\frac{2}{3} \div \frac{1}{4} =$

Answer:

QUESTION 4

An apprentice has $1\frac{2}{3}$ tubes of waterproof sealant. If the tubes are used on 3 separate jobs, how much will be used on each job? Express your answer as a fraction.

Answer:

QUESTION 5

A plumber has $2\frac{2}{3}$ bottles of inhibitor that are used on 2 jobs. How much is used on each job? Express your answer as a fraction.

Answer:

Unit 12: Percentages

Short-answer questions

Specific instructions to students

- In this unit, you will be able to practise and improve your skills in working out percentages.
- Read the following questions and answer all of them in the spaces provided.
- You need to show all working, you can use the blank Notes pages at the back of this book.

10% rule: Move the decimal one place to the left to get 10%.

EXAMPLE

10% of £45.00 would be £4.50

QUESTION 1

A repair bill for work on a hot water **cylinder**, including parts and labour, comes to £220. How much is 10% of the bill?

Answer:

_____

QUESTION 2

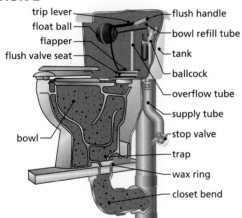

trip lever
float ball
flapper
flush valve seat
bowl

flush handle
bowl refill tube
tank
ballcock
overflow tube
supply tube
stop valve
trap
wax ring
closet bend

A toilet costs £249.

a   What is 10% of the cost?

Answer:

_____

b   How much will the toilet cost when this discount is subtracted from the initial cost?

Answer:

_____

QUESTION 3

Harry, the self-employed plumber, buys a new battery drill for £198.50. If he was given a 10% discount, how much did Harry pay for his new battery drill in total?

Answer:

_____

QUESTION 4

A plumber buys 5 l of central heating antifreeze for £84.80. A 5% discount is then given. How much is paid? (Hint: Find 10%, halve it and then subtract it from £84.80.)

Answer:

_____

QUESTION 5

Khan, the apprentice plumber, buys a new pipe slice for £14.99, a new pipe bending machine for £38.60 and an impact driver for £99.80.

a   How much has Khan spent on tools in total?

Answer:

_____

b   How much is paid after a 10% discount?

Answer:

_____

QUESTION 6

The following items are purchased for a workshop: a fluorescent light for £39.99, an adjustable spanner for £9.99, a socket set for £39.99, a digital thermometer for £12.99, a set of screwdrivers for £49.99 and a 25 m extension lead for £14.99.

a   How much is paid in total?

Answer:

_____

b   What is the final cost after a 10% discount?

Answer:

_____

QUESTION 7

A plumbing store offers 20% off the cost of screwdriver sets. If a set is priced at £36 before the discount, how much will each set cost after the discount?

Answer:

_____

QUESTION 8

Water pump pliers are discounted by 15%. If the recommended retail price for a set is £15.50 each, what is the discounted price?

Answer:

_____

QUESTION 9

Some new drill bits cost £16.90 as the regular retail price. The store then has a 20% sale. How much will the drill bits cost during the sale?

Answer:

_____

QUESTION 10

If an 18-volt battery drill costs £99, how much will it cost after the store takes off 30%?

Answer:

_____

Short-answer questions

Specific instructions to students

- This unit is designed to help you to improve your skills and increase your speed in converting one measurement into another.
- Read the following questions and answer all of them in the spaces provided.
- You need to show all working, you can use the blank Notes pages at the back of this book.

QUESTION 1

How many millimetres are there in 1 cm?

Answer:

_____

QUESTION 2

How many millimetres are there in 1 m?

Answer:

_____

QUESTION 3

How many centimetres are there in 1 m?

Answer:

_____

QUESTION 4

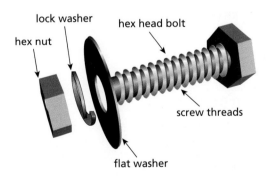

A coach bolt is 9 cm long. What is the bolt's length in millimetres (mm)?

Answer:

_____

QUESTION 5

How many millilitres are there in 4.8 l of tile adhesive?

Answer:

_____

QUESTION 6

How many litres are there in 3500 ml of drain cleaner?

Answer:

_____

QUESTION 7

A plumber's work van weighs $\frac{1}{2}$ a tonne. How many kilograms is that?

Answer:

_____

QUESTION 8

A builder's van weighs 2 tonnes. How many kilograms is that?

Answer:

_____

QUESTION 9

A small delivery van carrying piping weighs 4750 kg. How many tonnes does it weigh? Express your answer as a decimal.

Answer:

_____

QUESTION 10

A trailer measures 180 cm in length and 120 cm across the back. What is the **perimeter** of the trailer?

Answer:

_____

Unit 14: Measurement – Length, Area and Volume

Section A: Circumference

Short-answer questions

Specific instructions to students

- This section is designed to help you both to improve your skills and to increase your speed in measuring circumferences.
- Read the following questions and answer all of them in the spaces provided.
- You need to show all working, you can use the blank Notes pages at the back of this book.

$$C = \pi \times d$$

where: C = circumference, π = 3.14 and d = diameter.

EXAMPLE

Find the circumference of a pipe with a diameter of 30 cm.

$$C = \pi \times d$$

Therefore, $C = 3.14 \times 30$
$$= 94.2 \text{ cm}$$

QUESTION 1

What is the **circumference** of a boiler flue pipe with a diameter of 90 cm?

Answer:

QUESTION 2

Find the circumference of a **cold water mains** pipe with a diameter of 15 cm.

Answer:

QUESTION 3

Calculate the circumference of a drainage pipe with a diameter of 32 cm.

Answer:

QUESTION 4

What is the circumference of a washing machine hose with a diameter of 5 cm?

Answer:

QUESTION 5

Find the circumference of dish washer hose with a diameter of 12 cm.

Answer:

QUESTION 6

Calculate the circumference of an industrial heating pipe with a diameter of 28.8 cm.

Answer:

QUESTION 7

What is the circumference of a tin of flux with a diameter of 15.6 cm?

Answer:

QUESTION 8

Find the circumference of an angle grinder disc with a diameter of 14.3 cm.

Answer:

_____

QUESTION 9

Calculate the circumference of a toilet with a diameter of 42.9 cm.

Answer:

_____

QUESTION 10

Find the circumference of a sink with a diameter of 18.8 cm.

Answer:

_____

Section B: Diameter ⑫

Short-answer questions

Specific instructions to students

- This section is designed to help you both to improve your skills and to increase your speed in measuring the diameter of a round object.
- Read the following questions and answer all of them in the spaces provided.
- You need to show all working, you can use the blank Notes pages at the back of this book.

> **Diameter (D) of a circle** $= \dfrac{\text{circumference}}{\pi\ (3.14)}$

EXAMPLE

Find the diameter of a **sewer pipe** with a circumference of 80 cm.

$D = \dfrac{80}{3.14} = 25.48$ cm

QUESTION 1

What is the diameter of a sink with a circumference of 120 cm?

Answer:

_____

QUESTION 2

Find the diameter of an **LCS** (low carbon steel) flange with a circumference of 16 cm.

Answer:

_____

QUESTION 3

Calculate the diameter of a pipe with a circumference of 20 cm.

Answer:

_____

QUESTION 4

What is the diameter of a pipe sleeve with a circumference of 100 cm?

Answer:

_____

QUESTION 5

Find the diameter of a hot water cylinder with a circumference of 430 cm.

Answer:

_____

QUESTION 6

What is the diameter of an LCS union with a circumference of 11.8 cm?

Answer:

_____

QUESTION 7

Find the diameter of a combination boiler filling loop with a circumference of 12.4 cm.

Answer:

_____

QUESTION 8

Calculate the diameter of a soil pipe with a circumference of 90.8 cm.

Answer:

_____

QUESTION 9

What is the diameter of a round toilet bowl with a circumference of 102.3 cm?

Answer:

_____

QUESTION 10

Find the diameter of an **unvented** hot water cylinder with a circumference of 260.8 cm.

Answer:

_____

Section C: Area

Short-answer questions

Specific instructions to students

- This section is designed to help you both to improve your skills and to increase your speed in measuring surface area.
- Read the following questions and answer all of them in the spaces provided.
- You need to show all working, you can use the blank Notes pages at the back of this book.

> Area = length × width and is given in square
> units = *l* × *w*

QUESTION 1

A cold water **storage cistern** is 18 m × 1.2 m. What is the total base **area** of the tank?

Answer:

_____

QUESTION 2

Lucy the plumber is measuring the floor area of a bathroom that is to be floor tiled. The floor measures 60 m × 13 m. What is the total bathroom floor area?

Answer:

_____

QUESTION 3

If a sheet of plasterboard is 2.85 m × 1.65 m, what is the total area?

Answer:

_____

QUESTION 4

A welding space is 4.5 m × 1.8 m. What is the total area?

Answer:

_____

QUESTION 5

A roll of **sheet lead** can be purchased by the square metre. What is the total area of a 30 m roll that is 1.5 m wide?

Answer:

_____

QUESTION 6

If a shower wall that needs sealing measures 1.95 m × 0.98 m, what is the total area of the shower wall?

Answer:

_____

QUESTION 7

An apprentice plumber is to measure the floor of an existing bathroom to price for under-floor heating. The floor measures 106 m × 1.07 m. What is the total bathroom floor area?

Answer:

_____

QUESTION 8

An industrial plumbing storage area is 65.3 m × 32.7 m. How much floor area is there in total?

Answer:

_____

QUESTION 9

The dimensions of a floor area of a plumbing display at a DIY store measure 3.2 m × 8.6 m. What is the total floor area?

Answer:

_____

QUESTION 10

The protective tray in the back of a plumbing company's van has a side that is 8.9 m long and is 2.6 m wide. How much floor area can it accommodate?

Answer:

_____

Section D: Volume of a cube

Short-answer questions

Specific instructions to students

- This section is designed to help you both to improve your skills and to increase your speed in calculating volume of rectangular or square objects.
- Read the following questions and answer all of them in the spaces provided.
- You need to show all working, you can use the blank Notes pages at the back of this book.

> Volume of a cube = length × width × height and is given in cubic units
> = $l \times w \times h$

QUESTION 1
How many cubic metres are there in a storage area measuring 13 m × 5 m × 4 m?

Answer:

QUESTION 2
A pick up truck has the following dimensions: 8 m × 2 m × 3 m. How many cubic metres are available in the truck?

Answer:

QUESTION 3
If a trailer used for transporting plumbing materials is 18 m long × 3 m high × 3 m wide, how much **volume** can it hold?

Answer:

QUESTION 4
A welder constructs a small trailer for a plumber to store his tools in, measuring 2.2 m × 1.8 m × 0.5 m. How much volume can it hold?

Answer:

QUESTION 5

A plumber buys a new toolbox with the following dimensions: 0.6 m × 0.3 m × 0.15 m. How many cubic metres can the toolbox hold?

Answer:

QUESTION 6
A bathroom measures 1.5 m × 2.3 m × 2.1 m. What is its volume?

Answer:

QUESTION 7
A spare parts box is 1 m long, 0.6 m wide and 0.75 m tall. How much volume is available for storing parts?

Answer:

QUESTION 8

An indirect cold water supply, in a house, has a cold water storage cistern that is 1.4 m wide × 1.6 m long × 0.9 m high. What is its volume in cubic metres?

Answer:

_____

QUESTION 9

A plumber buys a new van that is 1.75 m high × 1.35 m wide × 3.6 m long. What is its volume in cubic metres?

Answer:

_____

QUESTION 10

An apprentice needs to paint a workshop's walls and floor that measure 3.8 m × 3.8 m × 2.5 m. How many cubic metres need to be painted?

Answer:

_____

Section E: Volume of a cylinder

Short-answer questions

Specific instructions to students

- This section is designed to help you both to improve your skills and to increase your speed in calculating volume of cylinder shaped objects.
- Read the following questions and answer all of them in the spaces provided.
- You need to show all working, you can use the blank Notes pages at the back of this book.

> Volume of a cylinder (V_c) = π (3.14) × r^2
> (radius × radius) × height
> $V_c = \pi \times r^2 \times h$

QUESTION 1

What is the volume of a drum that is filled with cleaning fluid and that has a **radius** of 0.4 m and a height of 1.4 m?

Answer:

_____

QUESTION 2

What is the volume of a cylinder of butane gas that has a radius of 3 cm and a height of 20 cm?

Answer:

_____

QUESTION 3

A hot water cylinder has a radius of 1.2 m and a height of 2 m. What is its volume?

Answer:

_____

QUESTION 4

A silicon gun has a radius of 3 cm and a length of 30 cm. How much grease can it hold?

Answer:

_____

QUESTION 5

A can of lubricant has a radius of 4 cm and a height of 20 cm. What is its volume?

Answer:

_____

QUESTION 6

A plumber's bottle of cleaning fluid has a radius of 5 cm and a height of 25 cm.

a   If the bottle was originally filled from a 4 l container, how much cleaning fluid has been used?

Answer:

_____

b   How much is left in the 4 l container?

Answer:

_____

QUESTION 7

A 5 l container of drain cleaner gets poured into 3 containers. Each container has a radius of 5 cm and a height of 20 cm.

a   What is the volume of each container?

Answer:

_____

b   What is the volume of all 3 containers in total?

Answer:

_____

c   How much is left in the 5 l container?

Answer:

_____

QUESTION 8

A container of barrier cream has a radius of 10 cm and a height of 15 cm.

a   What is its volume?

Answer:

_____

b   If half is used, how much is left?

Answer:

_____

QUESTION 9

A container of general purpose plaster has a radius of 10 cm and a height of 20 cm.

a   What is its volume?

Answer:

_____

b   If you use 1750 ml, how much is left?

Answer:

_____

QUESTION 10

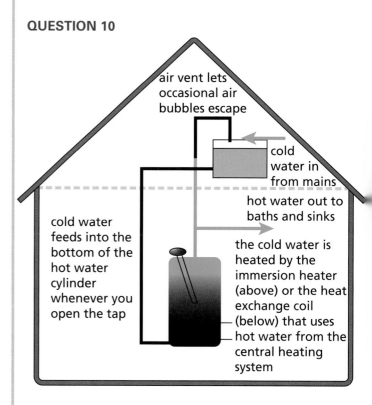

air vent lets occasional air bubbles escape

cold water in from mains

hot water out to baths and sinks

cold water feeds into the bottom of the hot water cylinder whenever you open the tap

the cold water is heated by the immersion heater (above) or the heat exchange coil (below) that uses hot water from the central heating system

A plumber installs a hot water cylinder with an immersion heater that has a radius of 1.2 m and is 3.6 m high. What is its volume in cubic metres?

Answer:

_____

Short-answer questions

Specific instructions to students

- This unit will help you to calculate both how much a job is worth and how long you need to complete the job.
- Read the following questions and answer all of them in the spaces provided.
- You need to show all working, you can use the blank Notes pages at the back of this book.

QUESTION 1

If a first-year plumbing apprentice earns £260.80 gross per week, how much does she earn per year?

Answer:

_____

QUESTION 2

A plumber starts work at 8.00 a.m. and stops for a break at 10.30 a.m. He begins to work again at 10.50 a.m. and finishes at 12.50 p.m. for lunch. He then resumes work at 2.00 p.m. and continues until 4.00 p.m. How many hours and minutes has he worked, excluding the breaks?

Answer:

_____

QUESTION 3

A second-year apprentice earns £15.50 per hour and works a 38-hour week. How much will her gross earnings be (before tax)?

Answer:

_____

QUESTION 4

Over a week, a plumber completes 5 jobs that amount to the following: £465.80, £2490.50, £556.20, £1560.70 and £990.60. What does the total bill come to?

Answer:

_____

QUESTION 5

A plumber needs to remove the following: piping (that takes 34 minutes); a tap (that takes 8 minutes); two tiles (that takes 7 minutes); the tiles around the vanity (that takes 24 minutes) and a door (that takes 9 minutes). How much time has been taken up in total on this job? State your answer in hours and minutes.

Answer:

_____

QUESTION 6

A 6 m length of copper pipe needs to be removed before being replaced. This takes the plumber $4\frac{1}{2}$ hours. If the rate of pay for labour is £28.60 per hour, how much will the plumber be paid for the time that he has worked?

Answer:

_____

QUESTION 7

A small plumbing job takes $1\frac{1}{2}$ hours to complete. If the plumber is getting paid £34.80 per hour, what is the total that she will earn?

Answer:

_____

QUESTION 8

A leak in a bathroom causes major damage. The bath tiles, floor tiles and shower tiles need to be removed before the plumber and his apprentice can begin the plumbing work. They spend 104 hours in total working on this job. If they work 8 hours per day, how many days will it take?

Answer:

QUESTION 9

A plumber begins work at 8.00 a.m. and works until 4.00 p.m. She spends 20 minutes on her morning break, 60 minutes on her lunch break and 20 minutes on her afternoon break.

a   How much time has been spent on breaks in total?

Answer:

---

b   How much time has she spent working?

Answer:

QUESTION 10

A job costs £550.50 to complete. The plumber spends 12 hours on the job. How much is his hourly rate?

Answer:

Unit 16: Squaring Numbers

Section A: Introducing square numbers

Any number squared is multiplied by itself.

EXAMPLE

4 squared $= 4^2 = 4 \times 4 = 16$

QUESTION 1

$6^2 =$

Answer:

QUESTION 2

$8^2 =$

Answer:

QUESTION 3

$12^2 =$

Answer:

QUESTION 4

$3^2 =$

Answer:

QUESTION 5

$7^2 =$

Answer:

QUESTION 6

$11^2 =$

Answer:

QUESTION 7

$10^2 =$

Answer:

QUESTION 8

$9^2 =$

Answer:

QUESTION 9

$2^2 =$

Answer:

QUESTION 10

$4^2 =$

Answer:

QUESTION 11

$5^2 =$

Answer:

Section B: Applying square numbers to the trade

Worded practical problems

Specific instructions to students

- This section is designed to help you both to improve your skills and to increase your speed in calculating the area of rectangular or square objects. The worded questions make the content relevant to everyday situations.
- Read the following questions and answer all of them in the spaces provided.
- You need to show all working, you can use the blank Notes pages at the back of this book.

QUESTION 1

A plumber measures an area that will be used for a water tank. The area measures 2.8 m × 2.8 m. What area does it take up?

Answer:

_____

QUESTION 2

A plumber's workshop has a work area that is 5.2 m × 5.2 m. What is the total area?

Answer:

_____

QUESTION 3

The dimensions of a bathroom that is to be re-plumbed are 12.6 m × 12.6 m. What is the total area?

Answer:

_____

QUESTION 4

A plumbing accessories showroom floor space measures 15 m². If there is an area allocated for the reception that is 2.4 m², how much floor space is left?

Answer:

_____

QUESTION 5

A plumbing warehouse has an area set aside for equipment that measures 13.8 m². If the spare parts area takes up 1.2 m² and the tool area is 2.7 m², how much area is left?

Answer:

_____

QUESTION 6

A plumber needs to remove and replace the floorboards in a bathroom that measures 2.4 m². If he removes 1.65m², how much of the floor area is left?

Answer:

_____

QUESTION 7

A plumber cuts out a piece of 5 cm × 5 cm plasterboard from a sheet that is 1.2 m². How much sheet area is left?

Answer:

_____

QUESTION 8

A tiled bathroom floor measures 28 m × 28 m. If it costs £9.50 to seal 1 m², how much will it cost to seal the whole floor?

Answer:

_____
_____

QUESTION 9

Each of the four walls of a workshop measures 2.6 m × 2.6 m. To insulate 1 m², it costs £28.50. How much will it cost to insulate all four walls?

Answer:

_____
_____
_____

QUESTION 10

Four walls of a workshop need to be painted. The total wall area measures 22 m². If it costs £6.80 to paint 1 m², how much will it cost to paint the 22 m²?

Answer:

_____

Unit 17: Ratios and Averages

Section A: Introducing ratios

Short-answer questions

Specific instructions to students

- This section is designed to help to improve your skills in calculating and simplifying **ratios**.
- Read the following questions and answer all of them in the spaces provided.
- Reduce the ratios to the simplest or lowest form.
- You need to show all working, you can use the blank Notes pages at the back of this book.

QUESTION 1

The number of teeth on gear cog 1 is 40. The number of teeth on gear cog 2 is 20. What is the ratio of gear cog 1 to gear cog 2?

Answer:

_____

QUESTION 2

Expansion vessel A has a diameter of 60 cm and vessel B has a diameter of 15 cm. What is the ratio of diameter A to B?

Answer:

_____

QUESTION 3

Rainwater pipe A has a diameter of 48 cm and rainwater pipe B has a diameter of 16 cm. What is the ratio of diameter A to B?

Answer:

_____

QUESTION 4

Two large hacksaws have 750 and 150 teeth. What is the ratio of the teeth on the blades?

Answer:

_____

QUESTION 5

Three cogs have 80, 60 and 20 teeth. What is the ratio?

Answer:

_____

QUESTION 6

A lathe has 2 pulleys that have diameters of 16 cm and 20 cm. What is the lower ratio?

Answer:

_____

QUESTION 7

The diameter of pulley A on a bandsaw is 32 cm. Pulley B has a diameter of 16 cm and pulley C has a diameter of 48 cm. What is the lowest ratio of the three compared together?

Answer:

_____

QUESTION 8

Three sewer pipes have different diameters: 18 cm, 16 cm and 10 cm. What is the comparative ratio?

Answer:

_____

QUESTION 9

Circular saw A has a diameter of 34 cm and circular saw B has a diameter of 12 cm. What is the ratio?

Answer:

_____

QUESTION 10

The circumference of pipe A is 62 cm and the circumference of pipe B is 38 cm. What is the ratio?

Answer:

_____

Section B: Applying ratios to the trade

Short-answer questions

Specific instructions to students

- This section is designed to help you to improve your practical skills when working with **ratios**.
- Read the following questions and answer all of them in the spaces provided.
- You need to show all working, you can use the blank Notes pages at the back of this book.

QUESTION 1

The ratio of the teeth on cog 1 to cog 2 is 3 : 1. If cog 2 has 10 teeth, how many teeth will cog 1 have?

Answer:

_____

QUESTION 2

The ratio of the teeth on hacksaw 1 to hacksaw 2 is 2 : 1. If hacksaw 2 has 200 teeth, how many teeth will hacksaw 1 have?

Answer:

_____

QUESTION 3

The ratio of the diameter of flue pipe A to flue pipe B is 4 : 2. If flue pipe A has a diameter of 40 cm, what will be the diameter of flue pipe B?

Answer:

_____

QUESTION 4

The ratio of the diameter of pipe A to pipe B is 2 : 1. If pipe A has a diameter of 30 cm, what will be the diameter of pipe B?

Answer:

_____

QUESTION 5

The ratio of teeth on jigsaw A to jigsaw B is 3 : 1. If the number of teeth on jigsaw A is 12, how many teeth are on jigsaw B?

Answer:

_____

QUESTION 6

The ratio of males and females joining plumbing apprenticeships is 2 : 1 respectively. If the number of males undertaking plumbing apprenticeships over the past month is 18, how many females joined apprenticeships last month?

Answer:

_____

QUESTION 7

The ratio of gas engineers using boiler A to boiler B is 3 : 1. If the number of gas engineers using boiler A is 21, how many gas engineers prefer boiler B?

Answer:

QUESTION 8

The ratio of expansion of pipe A to pipe B when hot is 3 : 2. If pipe A expands 6 mm, how much will pipe B expand?

Answer:

QUESTION 9

The ratio of plumbers using flux A to flux B is 4 : 3 respectively. Sixteen plumbers use brand A. How many plumbers use brand B?

Answer:

QUESTION 10

The ratio of teeth on circular saw A to circular saw B is 4 : 3. If circular saw A has 240 teeth, how many teeth will circular saw B have?

Answer:

Section C: Mean, median, mode and range

Short-answer questions

Specific instructions to students

- This section will help you to improve your skills when working with averages.
- The **mean**, **median**, **mode** and **range** are all types of average. Read the definitions, study the examples and then complete the table.
- You need to show all working, you can use the blank Notes pages at the back of this book.

Definition	Example series: 2, 2, 4, 4, 6, 8, 10, 12	Find the averages for the following series: 4, 4, 6, 10, 12, 14, 16, 18, 20, 20
THE MEAN To find the **mean**, you need to add up all the data, and then divide this total by the number of values in the data.	Adding the numbers up gives: $2 + 2 + 4 + 4 + 6 + 8 + 10 + 12 = 52$ There are 8 values, so divide the total by 8: $48 \div 8 = 6$ **So the mean is 6**	
THE MEDIAN To find the **median**, you need to put the values in order, and then find the middle value. If there are two values in the middle, then you find the mean of these two values.	The numbers in order 2, 2, 4, **4**, **6**, 8, 10, 12 The middle values are in bold. $4 + 6 = 10$ $10 \div 2 = 5$ **So the median is 5**	
THE MODE The **mode** is the value that appears the most often in the data. It is possible to have more than one mode if there is more than one value that appears the most.	The data values 2, 2, 4, 4, 6, 8, 10, 12 The values that appear most often are 2 and 4. They both appear more times than any other data values. **So the modes are 2 and 4**	
THE RANGE To find the **range**, you first need to find the lowest and highest values in the data. The range is found by subtracting the lowest value from the highest value.	The data values 2, 2, 4, 4, 6, 8, 10, 12 The lowest value is 2 and the highest value is 12. $12 - 2 = 10$ **So the range is 10**	

Unit 18: Pythagoras' Theorem

Short-answer questions

Specific instructions to students

- This unit is designed to help you to improve your skills in calculating measurement and area using Pythagoras' theorem.
- Read the following questions and answer all of them in the spaces provided.
- You need to show all working, you can use the blank Notes pages at the back of this book.

The following theorem applies to right-angled triangles, which are often encountered by workers in the plumbing industry.

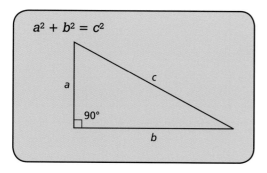

If we consider this formula as it applies to the plumbing trade, we can introduce the following terms.

a = side length 'a' (or **run**)

b = side length 'b' (or offset)

c = diagonal length

a (run)   90°   c (diagonal)   b (offset)

So if:

$a^2 + b^2 = c^2$

then to solve for c (the diagonal length), you need to find the square root of $a^2 + b^2$.

To solve Questions 1–3, you will need to refer to the following example.

A plumber knows that side a is 2 m long and that side b is at a right angle to side a. He also knows that side b measures 3 m. He needs to fit a length of pipe to the diagonal side; however, he doesn't know the length of the diagonal. What is the length of the diagonal, c?

$$a^2 + b^2 = c^2$$
$$2^2 + 3^2 = c^2$$
$$4 + 9 = c^2$$
$$13 = c^2$$
$$\sqrt{13} = c$$
$$3.6 = c$$

Therefore, the pipe needs to measure 3.61 m for the diagonal length c.

QUESTION 1

If side a is 3 m and side b is 3 m, what is the length of the diagonal side c that needs to be cut?

Answer:

Answer:

QUESTION 2

If side a is 1 m and side b is 3 m, what is the length of the diagonal side c that needs to be cut?

Answer:

QUESTION 3

If side a is 4 m and side b is 5 m, what is the length of the diagonal side c that needs to be cut?

Unit 19: Mechanical Reasoning

Short-answer questions

Specific instructions to students

- This unit is designed to help you improve your skills in mechanical reasoning.
- Read the following questions and answer all of them in the spaces provided.
- You will need to show all working. Use the blank Notes pages at the back of the book.

QUESTION 1

If cog X turns in a clockwise direction, which way will cog Y turn?

Answer:

QUESTION 2

If pulley A turns in a clockwise direction, which way will pulley D turn?

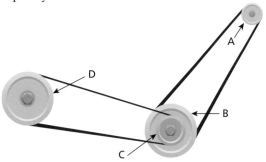

Answer:

QUESTION 3

If the drive pulley in the following diagram of a work van engine turns in a clockwise direction, in which direction will the alternator turn?

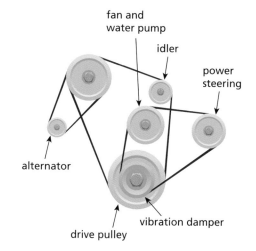

Answer:

QUESTION 4

Looking at the following diagram, if lever A moves to the left, in which direction will lever B move?

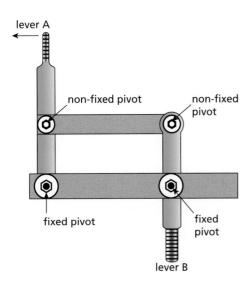

Answer:

QUESTION 5

In the following diagram, pully 1 turns clockwise. In which direction will pulley 6 turn?

Answer:

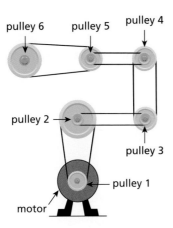

QUESTION 6

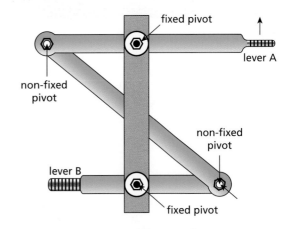

If lever A is pulled up, what will happen to lever B?

Answer:

Unit 20: Reading, Interpreting and Understanding Data

The Health and Safety at Work Act 1974 is the principal piece of legislation covering work based health and safety requirements. Below is a chart showing the most common types of work based injuries. From the given data answer the following questions.

Causes of Injuries Percentage

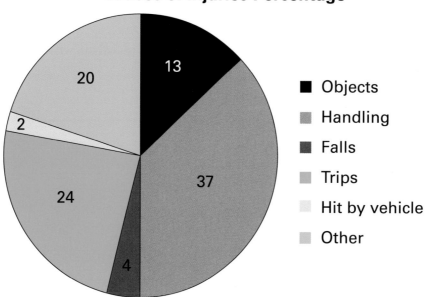

- ■ Objects
- ■ Handling
- ■ Falls
- ■ Trips
- ■ Hit by vehicle
- ■ Other

QUESTION 1

What is the name given to the above type of chart?

Answer:

_____

QUESTION 2

What is the most common cause of injuries?

Answer:

_____

QUESTION 3

What percentage of injuries does the most common cause make up?

Answer:

_____

QUESTION 4

What percentage of injuries is caused by trips?

Answer:

_____

QUESTION 5

20% of injuries are designated 'other'. Name some things you consider that 'other' could be.

Answer:

_____

QUESTION 6

Using the data above, draw a bar chart showing all the details and percentages.

Answer:

QUESTION 7

Using the data above, draw a line graph showing all the details and percentages.

Answer:

Unit 21
Practice Written Exam for the Plumbing Trade

Reading time: 10 minutes

Writing time: 1 hour 30 minutes

Section A: English

Section B: Mathematics

QUESTION and ANSWER BOOK

Section	Topic	Number of questions	Marks
A	English	10	90
B	Mathematics	14	40
		Total 24	Total 130

The sections may be completed in the order of your choice.

Task 1: Job application

10 marks

Brentwood Plumbing Services

We require a trainee plumber to join our installation team!

Full training will be provided in all aspects of the plumbing industry.

If you are looking to enter the plumbing industry and are enthusiastic and hard-working, then do not hesitate to contact us today!

Contact:
Alan Brentwood,
Brentwood Plumbing Services,
106 Main Road Industrial Estate,
Leeds Road,
Newtown,
Lancashire OH5 7BD

You have seen this advertisement in your local newspaper and you would like to apply for the trainee position. The company is well established and has an excellent reputation.

Write a letter of application to the company, providing full personal details. You should include:
* why you would like to work for the company
* all relevant qualifications
* what experience you have; this could be any work experience or voluntary work
* what skills and experience you could bring to the company
* why you want to be a plumber.

You should:
* use the correct letter format
* write in full sentences
* use correct spelling, punctuation and grammar

Remember: plan your letter of application before you write your draft and final letter.

Answer:

Task 2: Car auction L1

10 marks

You are placing an advert on an auction website to sell your car. Write a full and honest description, highlighting all of the good points that will persuade someone to bid on your item. Think carefully about:
• the tone and language you use, to make your item sound appealing to potential customers
• making sure your description is clear and concise
• the use of fact and opinion in your description.

Answer:

Task 3: Cover letter

Rhia has written in response to the advertisement that she spotted in her local newspaper, shown below.

Plumber

Required for local contract. Must have two years' experience.

Please send your CV and covering letter, to:

Jenny Clucas

Red34 at Ledbury

Harley Drive

Ledbury

She has asked you to look over her covering letter before she posts it to see if she has included all the relevant points. She has also asked if you can help her write it again, if necessary.

Hi there

I want the job you've put in the local newspaper this week. I've been in plumbing for 2 years and I can get people to vouch for me, if you want. Here's a list of my qualifications and where I've worked before, in with this letter.

You can call me on 07562 725094.

Rhia

Help Rhia by rewriting the short covering letter to accompany her CV, using the correct structure, content and layout for a formal covering letter.

Answer:

Task 4: Flyers

Specialist Tool Centre
Crazy! Crazy! Spring sale!

The Specialist Tool Centre is leading the way in tool discount madness; yes, we are giving all our customers up to 30% discount on our full range of high quality power tools!

Yes, you will be amazed at how low our prices are for all, yes all, our latest high quality battery drills, impact drivers, diamond core drills, core drills and many, many more items!

You will be amazed, thrilled and staggered at how low our prices are; so don't delay! Come and visit us today.

Offer open for one week only!

Specialist Tool Centre, Unit 5 North Road Park, Elton, Lancashire.
Tel.: 0164 755 67774
www.specialisttoolcentre.com

You have been given a flyer for the Specialist Tool Centre spring sale.

QUESTION 1   1 mark

Which of the following statements best describes the purpose of the flyer?
(1) To criticize
(2) To assess
(3) To advertise
(4) To review

Answer:

QUESTION 2   4 marks

The flyer has been designed to give maximum impact and promote the sale. List four high impact words used in the advertisement.

Answer:

You are the owner of a successful gardening business and would like to attract more customers who would like to have their garden buildings maintained. Produce a flyer for your business using high impact words to maximize the impact of the flyer.

Answer:

Task 5: Help from a friend   **22 marks**

You have set up as a self-employed plumber and become successful. You now want to expand your business, but need some help.

Your task is to write an email to a friend asking for help distributing flyers to the local area (residential and business addresses).

Your friend's email address is nick.bailey@thebaileys.co.uk

It would be good to expand on the following points:
- your reason for writing
- why you are excited and what expanding the business will mean to you
- details of what you want your friend to do
- why you have chosen him to help you
- making arrangements to meet up and discuss what you will do.

Answer:

Task 6: New home build 12 marks

Your local council is to have a meeting to decide if a large building company can be granted planning permission to build 150 new homes on green belt land in the community. If planning permission is granted, it will have an immediate impact on local resources such as schools and hospitals, and cause increases in traffic and pollution. There are no plans to improve any local services to accommodate the growth in the local population.

Your task is to write a formal letter to the local planning department to complain about the proposed new houses and their effect on the local community. The person to write to is: Michael Jones, Head of Planning, Planning House, Taylor Street, Newbury NN12 6TY.

In your letter, you must include the following points:
*   The main issue
*   Who will be affected
*   The effect on the local community
*   Why you want to oppose the new house build.

Answer:

Task 7: New bathroom showroom 6 marks

MODERN BATHROOMS LTD

Announce the opening of our brand new showroom on Bank Holiday Monday at 9.00 a.m.!

We have a large display of bathrooms, showers and hot tubs!

Come and have a look around and be amazed at our low prices!!

22 Main Street, Southtown, Lancashire SHU 4RT

www.modernbathrooms.com

Above is an advertisement for the opening of a new bathroom showroom. Answer the following questions:

a   Which day will the new showroom open?

_____

b   What will be on display in the showroom?

_____

c   Why will customers be amazed?

_____

d   What time will the new showroom open?

_____

e   What is the company name?

_____

f   What is the company web address?

_____

Task 8: Trainee plumber

Job description

You will be working for an established plumbing and heating company. You will have the opportunity to train as an apprentice plumber in a full-time role where you will perform basic duties to begin with.

Your role will include:
- attending training as required
- helping a qualified plumber on site
- meeting and greeting customers
- observing and learning
- tidying the work area.

Working week

You will be required to work Monday–Friday and some Saturdays if required, with one day a week (Tuesday) attending college (39-hour week including training).

Training to be provided

You will receive high levels of training and support while on the job. You will be working towards the NVQ Level 2 apprenticeship in plumbing at a local college on a day-release basis undertaking theory and practical tuition. This will be in addition to on-the-job training with an experienced plumber.

Qualifications required

Ideally candidates should have GCSE (or equivalent) Maths and English at minimum grade C or above, or Functional Skills in Maths and English Level 1. Candidates that have not achieved the entry-level requirements will be required to undertake an assessment interview, and it will only be on successful completion of the assessment that they will be accepted on to the course. All candidates will be required to undertake Functional Skills as part of the training to a minimum of Level 1.

Skills required

Good communication skills and ability to work in a team. Candidates should be able to interact with staff and customers alike.

Personal qualities required

Pleasant and honest disposition, as you will be dealing with the general public.

QUESTION 1   8 marks

a   According to the text, which day is spent at college?

Answer:

_____

b   According to the text, what other day may have to be worked?

Answer:

_____

c   Name three basic duties required to be undertaken.

Answer:

_____

_____

_____

d   Using a dictionary, explain these words: *Communication, Interact, Apprentice, Assessment.*

Answer:

Communication: _____

_____

Interact: _____

_____

Apprentice: _____

_____

Assessment: _____

_____

e   What qualifications are ideal for the job?

Answer:

_____

_____

f   What skills are required for the job?

Answer:

_____

_____

g   How many days a week would be spent at college?

Answer:

_____

h   What qualifications will be undertaken while at college?

Answer:

_____

_____

Task 1

You have completed your apprenticeship in plumbing and are celebrating at home by inviting friends round for a takeaway meal. You want to order an Indian meal for a total of 6 people from the selection available:

Meal number	Type of food	Meal feeds	Price of meal
001	vegetarian dishes	one person	£5.40
002	meat dishes	one person	£5.60
003	fish dishes	one person	£5.80
004	vegetarian dishes	two people	£9.20
005	meat dishes	two people	£9.40
006	fish dishes	two people	£9.80
007	vegetarian dishes	three people	£13.60
008	meat dishes	three people	£14.00
009	fish dishes	three people	£14.40
010	vegetarian dishes	four people	£17.40
011	meat dishes	four people	£17.60
012	fish dishes	four people	£18.20

You must decide what meals to order for your friends and yourself to eat.

QUESTION 1   2 marks

List the meal numbers, type of food and cost of each selection.

Answer:

_____

_____

_____

QUESTION 2   2 marks

What is the total cost of the meal for 6 people? Show your working out.

Answer:

_____

_____

QUESTION 3   3 marks

The takeaway offers a 15% discount for telephone orders. How much money will you get off your food order? Show your working out and answer using the correct format for money.

Answer:

_____

_____

_____

QUESTION 4   2 marks

What is the total amount payable with the discount applied to your food order? Show your working out and use the correct format for money.

Answer:

_____

_____

QUESTION 5   5 marks

Draw a table to show your order including the following important information:
- set meal numbers
- quantity of each meal ordered
- price before discount applied
- amount of discount for each set meal
- cost of each set meal with discount applied
- total amount payable.

Answer:

QUESTION 6   **2 marks**

Your friends agree to share the cost of the takeaway food equally. How much will each person pay? Show your working out.

Answer:

_____

_____

QUESTION 7   **2 marks**

You phone for your takeaway at 7.20 p.m. and the order should arrive in a quarter of an hour. What time will the food be delivered?

Answer:

_____

_____

QUESTION 8   **2 marks**

Double-check at least one calculation from those listed above.

Answer:

_____

_____

_____

Task 2

This task is about the time that it takes two teams of plumbers to complete their jobs on a given day.

You are the supervisor and have set a target of 6.1 hours per job for each team member. The teams recorded how long they took to complete their jobs and the information is as follows:

Team 1		Team 2	
Bob	5.5 hrs	Luke	5.75 hrs
Bill	1.5 hrs	Chris	6.5 hrs
Eddie	6 hrs 30 mins	George	9 hrs
Harry	7 hrs 30 mins	Tyler	9 hrs 30 mins
Larry	6 hrs 10 mins	Richard	8 hrs
Tommy	6 hrs 50 mins	Bradley	5 hrs 15 mins
Nathan	3.5 hrs	Peter	8 hrs 45 mins
Charlie	6 hrs 30 mins	Ken	7 hrs 10 mins
Alex	5 hrs 50 mins		
Sam	7.25 hrs		

QUESTION 1   **3 marks**

What percentage of plumbers spends more than 6.1 hours completing jobs? Show your working out.

Answer:

_____

## QUESTION 2											5 marks

What are the mean numbers of hours spent completing jobs for the following? Show your answers in decimal format not in time format. Show your working out.

Answer:

_____

_____

_____

## QUESTION 3											5 marks

Draw a suitable chart on the graph paper provided opposite to show the mean number of hours spent completing jobs for Team 1, Team 2, the combined teams and also show the target set of 6.1 hours.

Answer:

_____

_____

_____

_____

_____

_____

## QUESTION 4											3 marks

What is the range of times spent completing jobs for the following? Show your working out and your answer in decimal format.

Answer:

_____

_____

_____

## QUESTION 5											2 marks

Comment on the results of the survey and the target set for completing jobs. Include one comment about the mean numbers and one comment about the ranges.

Answer:

_____

_____

_____

_____

_____

_____

_____

_____

## QUESTION 6											2 marks

Check one of your calculations using reverse calculation method. Show your working out.

Answer:

_____

_____

_____

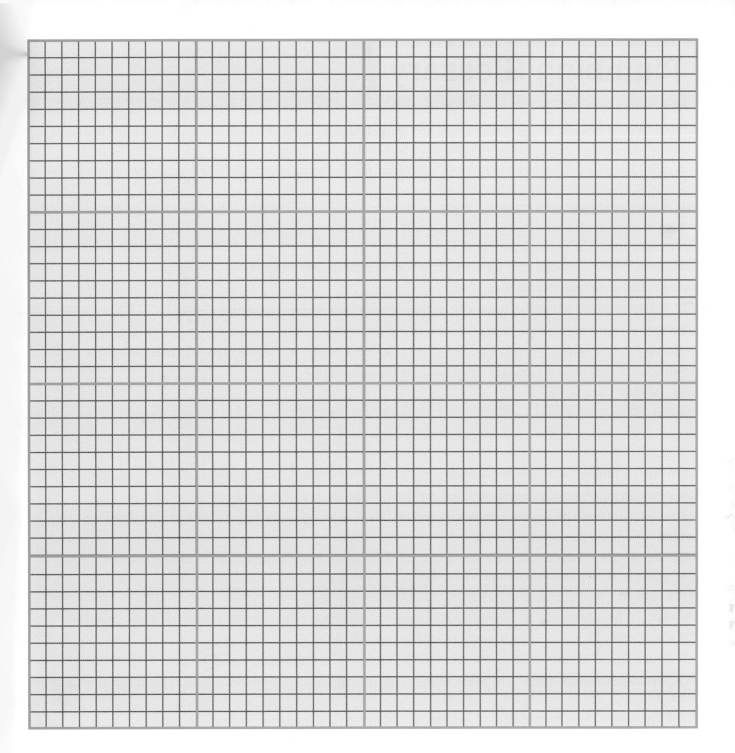

Plumbing Glossary

Acrylic A thermoplastic that is heat activated and is used on surfaces, such as baths. It comes in sheets and has a fibreglass backing that helps to form waterproof shower walls.

Ballcock The valve that controls the flow of water from the line of the water supply into a gravity operated toilet tank. A float mechanism controls the tank water.

CHP (Combined heat and power) A plant where electricity is generated and the excess heat generated is used for heating.

Circumference The perimeter of a circle.

Cistern A vessel for storing cold water that is subject to atmospheric pressure.

Closet A term that can be used for a toilet.

Cold water mains A pipe that carries the supply of fresh wholesome water to dwellings.

Cylinder A vessel used for the storage of hot water in a dwelling.

Diameter A line passing through the centre of a circle, extending from one side of the circumference to the other.

Drainpipe A pipe used to transport rainwater from the gutter to the drain.

Drop Vertical distance down.

Effluent Septic system liquid waste.

Elbow A pipe fitting with two openings that changes the direction of the line. It can come in a variety of angles, from 22.5° to 90°.

Estimate A costing for a piece of work that is not a fixed price but can go up or down.

Flue pipe A pipe from a gas appliance used to extract the products of combustion.

Grade The difference in degrees between the run and drop. It can allow for water to run off into a drain or trap.

Hazard Anything that can cause harm.

Heat exchanger A device that allows heat to be transferred from one water system to another without the two water systems coming into contact with each other.

Hydrocarbon A combination of hydrogen and carbon atoms.

Inhibitor A liquid made up of various chemicals used to stop the corrosion process in central heating systems.

JCB excavator A powerful machine for removing earth and soil.

LCS (low carbon steel) Steel used in a type of pipe for commercial heating installations.

LPG (liquid petroleum gas) The name for the family of carbon based gases that are found in coal and oil deposits underground.

MDPE (medium density polythene ethylene) Material used for a cold water mains pipe.

Natural gas A hydrocarbon fuel found naturally where oil and coal has formed underground.

O-ring A round rubber washer used to create a watertight seal, chiefly around valve stems.

Perimeter The length of a boundary around a shape.

PPE (personal protective equipment) Any piece of equipment worn by a person to create a barrier against workplace hazards.

Pressure relief valve A safety valve that safeguards against over-pressurization by allowing excess water pressure to discharge safely.

Pressure switch A device used on a central heating boiler that detects negative and positive pressure.

PVC (polyvinyl chloride) A material used for pipes in plumbing systems.

Radiator A heat emitter used in central heating systems.

Radius The shortest distance from the centre of a circle to the circumference.

Rainwater cycle A natural process where water is continually exchanged between the atmosphere, surface water, ground water and plants.

Risk assessment A detailed examination of any factor that could cause injury.

Run The horizontal distance usually along the ground and / or floor.

SEDBUK The seasonal efficiency of domestic boilers in the UK.

Service pipe A pipe that connects the external stop valve to a dwelling.

Sewer pipe   A conduit used to collect waste water and discharge it away from a dwelling.

Sheet lead   A hazardous non-ferrous metal used to weather buildings.

Soil pipe   A pipe used for the removal of waste water from sanitary equipment in a dwelling.

Storage cistern   A vessel designed to hold a supply of cold water to feed appliances fitted to the system.

System boiler   A central heating boiler that contains an expansion vessel and pressure relief valve in a single unit.

Unvented   The specification of a hot water system fed directly from the cold water mains and not open to the atmosphere, containing an expansion vessel.

WC cistern   A vessel used to flush a WC.

English Glossary

Adjective   A type of word that describes NOUNS (things, people and places), for example *sharp*, *warm* or *handsome*.

Adverb   A type of word that describes VERBS (things happening), for example *slowly*, *often* or *quickly*.

Apostrophe   A PUNCTUATION mark with two main functions: (1) shows where letters have been missed out when words or phrases are shortened, for example changing *cannot* to *can't*, or *I will* to *I'll*; (2) shows where a NOUN 'possesses' something, for example *Dave's bike*, *the cat's whiskers* or *St John's Wood*.

Capital letter   Used to begin a SENTENCE, to begin the names of people, days, months and places, and for abbreviations such as *RSPCA* or *FBI*.

Comma   A PUNCTUATION mark that has many uses, usually to separate phrases in a long SENTENCE so that it is easier to read and understand, or to separate items in a list.

Formal language   The type of language used when speaking to or writing to someone you don't know, such as your bank manager (e.g. 'I am writing to request a bank statement').

Full stop   A PUNCTUATION mark used at the end of SENTENCES.

Future tense   The VERB forms we use to talk about things that will happen in future (e.g. 'I *will watch* television tonight').

Homophone   A word that sounds the same as another word, but has a different spelling and meaning, for example *break* and *brake*.

Informal language   The type of language used when you are speaking to or writing to someone you know well, such as a friend (e.g. 'Hi, how are you? Do you fancy coming to the cinema with me?').

Instructions   A series or list of statements designed to show someone how to do something, for example to use some equipment or to follow some rules.

Noun   A word used to refer to a thing, person or place, for example *chair*, *George* or *Sheffield*.

Paragraph   A section of writing about the same subject or topic, that begins on a new line and consists of one or more SENTENCES.

Past tense   The VERB forms we use to talk about things that have happened in the past (e.g. 'I *watched* television last night').

Present tense   The VERB forms we use to talk about things that are happening now (e.g. 'I *am watching* television').

Pronouns   Words that are used instead of NOUNS (things, people and places), for example *he*, *she*, *we*, *it*, *who*, *something*, *ourselves*.

Punctuation   Marks used in writing to help make it clear and organized, by separating or joining together words or phrases, or by adding or changing emphasis.

Question mark   A PUNCTUATION mark used at the end of a question, to show that you have asked something.

Sentence   A group of words, beginning with a CAPITAL LETTER and ending with a FULL STOP, QUESTION MARK or exclamation mark, put together using correct grammar, to make a meaningful statement or question, etc.

Verb   Word used to indicate an action, for example *mix*, *smile* or *walk*.

Mathematics Glossary

Actual   The exact calculation of a set of numbers.

Analogue clock   A clock that displays minute and hour hands and shows the time changing continuously.

Area   The size of a surface; the amount of space in a two-dimensional shape or property, e.g. the floor space of a room or flat.

Decimal   A way of organizing numbers based around the number ten (the most familiar system used in the world today).

Decimal point   A mark, often a full stop, used in a number to divide between whole numbers and FRACTIONS of whole numbers shown in DECIMAL form.

Digital clock   A clock that tells the time using numbers instead of hands and shows the time changing digitally – from one exact value to the next.

Estimate   (1) A calculation that requires a rough guess rather than working out the actual figure; (2) to work out this value.

Fraction   A quantity or amount that is not a whole number, e.g. less than 1. A part of a whole number.

Imperial   The British system of units for weights and measures before the METRIC system, including pounds, stones, miles, feet and inches.

Mean   A form of average of a set of numbers. To calculate the mean, add all of the numbers together and then divide by how many numbers there are.

Median   A form of average of a set of numbers. To calculate the median, place the numbers in numerical order and then find the middle number.

Metric   An international DECIMAL system of units for weights and measures, including kilograms, grams, kilometres, metres and centimetres.

Mode   A form of average of a set of numbers. To calculate the mode, look for the number that appears most often.

Percentage   A proportion, or FRACTION, that means part of one hundred.

Perimeter   The total lengths of all of the sides of a two-dimensional shape or AREA, e.g. the distance around the outside of a room.

Range   The difference between the largest and smallest numbers in a set of figures.

Ratio   A way to compare the amounts of things – how much of one thing there is compared to how much of another thing.

Scales   An instrument used to measure the weight of an object or person.

Volume   The amount of three-dimensional space that an object occupies.

Formulae and Data

Circumference of a Circle

$C = \pi \times d$
where: C = circumference, π = 3.14, d = diameter

Diameter of a Circle

Diameter (d) of a circle $= \dfrac{\text{circumference}}{\pi \ (3.14)}$

Area

Area = length × breadth and is given in square units
$\quad = l \times b$

Volume of a Cube

Volume of a cube = length × width × height and is given in cubic units
$\quad\quad\quad = l \times w \times h$

Volume of a Cylinder

Volume of cylinder (V_c) = π (3.14) × r^2 (radius × radius) × height
$\quad\quad\quad V_c = \pi \times r^2 \times h$

Pythagoras' Theorem

$a^2 + b^2 = c^2$

Times Tables

1

1 × 1	=	1
2 × 1	=	2
3 × 1	=	3
4 × 1	=	4
5 × 1	=	5
6 × 1	=	6
7 × 1	=	7
8 × 1	=	8
9 × 1	=	9
10 × 1	=	10
11 × 1	=	11
12 × 1	=	12

2

1 × 2	=	2
2 × 2	=	4
3 × 2	=	6
4 × 2	=	8
5 × 2	=	10
6 × 2	=	12
7 × 2	=	14
8 × 2	=	16
9 × 2	=	18
10 × 2	=	20
11 × 2	=	22
12 × 2	=	24

3

1 × 3	=	3
2 × 3	=	6
3 × 3	=	9
4 × 3	=	12
5 × 3	=	15
6 × 3	=	18
7 × 3	=	21
8 × 3	=	24
9 × 3	=	27
10 × 3	=	30
11 × 3	=	33
12 × 3	=	36

4

1 × 4	=	4
2 × 4	=	8
3 × 4	=	12
4 × 4	=	16
5 × 4	=	20
6 × 4	=	24
7 × 4	=	28
8 × 4	=	32
9 × 4	=	36
10 × 4	=	40
11 × 4	=	44
12 × 4	=	48

5

1 × 5	=	5
2 × 5	=	10
3 × 5	=	15
4 × 5	=	20
5 × 5	=	25
6 × 5	=	30
7 × 5	=	35
8 × 5	=	40
9 × 5	=	45
10 × 5	=	50
11 × 5	=	55
12 × 5	=	60

6

1 × 6	=	6
2 × 6	=	12
3 × 6	=	18
4 × 6	=	24
5 × 6	=	30
6 × 6	=	36
7 × 6	=	42
8 × 6	=	48
9 × 6	=	54
10 × 6	=	60
11 × 6	=	66
12 × 6	=	72

7

1 × 7	=	7
2 × 7	=	14
3 × 7	=	21
4 × 7	=	28
5 × 7	=	35
6 × 7	=	42
7 × 7	=	49
8 × 7	=	56
9 × 7	=	63
10 × 7	=	70
11 × 7	=	77
12 × 7	=	84

8

1 × 8	=	8
2 × 8	=	16
3 × 8	=	24
4 × 8	=	32
5 × 8	=	40
6 × 8	=	48
7 × 8	=	56
8 × 8	=	64
9 × 8	=	72
10 × 8	=	80
11 × 8	=	88
12 × 8	=	96

9

1 × 9	=	9
2 × 9	=	18
3 × 9	=	27
4 × 9	=	36
5 × 9	=	45
6 × 9	=	54
7 × 9	=	63
8 × 9	=	72
9 × 9	=	81
10 × 9	=	90
11 × 9	=	99
12 × 9	=	108

10

1 × 10	=	10
2 × 10	=	20
3 × 10	=	30
4 × 10	=	40
5 × 10	=	50
6 × 10	=	60
7 × 10	=	70
8 × 10	=	80
9 × 10	=	90
10 × 10	=	100
11 × 10	=	110
12 × 10	=	120

11

1 × 11	=	11
2 × 11	=	22
3 × 11	=	33
4 × 11	=	44
5 × 11	=	55
6 × 11	=	66
7 × 11	=	77
8 × 11	=	88
9 × 11	=	99
10 × 11	=	110
11 × 11	=	121
12 × 11	=	132

12

1 × 12	=	12
2 × 12	=	24
3 × 12	=	36
4 × 12	=	48
5 × 12	=	60
6 × 12	=	72
7 × 12	=	84
8 × 12	=	96
9 × 12	=	108
10 × 12	=	120
11 × 12	=	132
12 × 12	=	144

Multiplication Grid

	1	2	3	4	5	6	7	8	9	10	11	12
1	1	2	3	4	5	6	7	8	9	10	11	12
2	2	4	6	8	10	12	14	16	18	20	22	24
3	3	6	9	12	15	18	21	24	27	30	33	36
4	4	8	12	16	20	24	28	32	36	40	44	48
5	5	10	15	20	25	30	35	40	45	50	55	60
6	6	12	18	24	30	36	42	48	54	60	66	72
7	7	14	21	28	35	42	49	56	63	70	77	84
8	8	16	24	32	40	48	56	64	72	80	88	96
9	9	18	27	36	45	54	63	72	81	90	99	108
10	10	20	30	40	50	60	70	80	90	100	110	120
11	11	22	33	44	55	66	77	88	99	110	121	132
12	12	24	36	48	60	72	84	96	108	120	132	144

Maths & English for Plumbing
Online Answer Guide

To access the Answer Guide for Maths & English for Plumbing follow these simple steps:

1) Copy the following link into your web browser:

http://www.cengagebrain.co.uk/shop/isbn/9781408083109

2) Click on the Free Study Tools link.

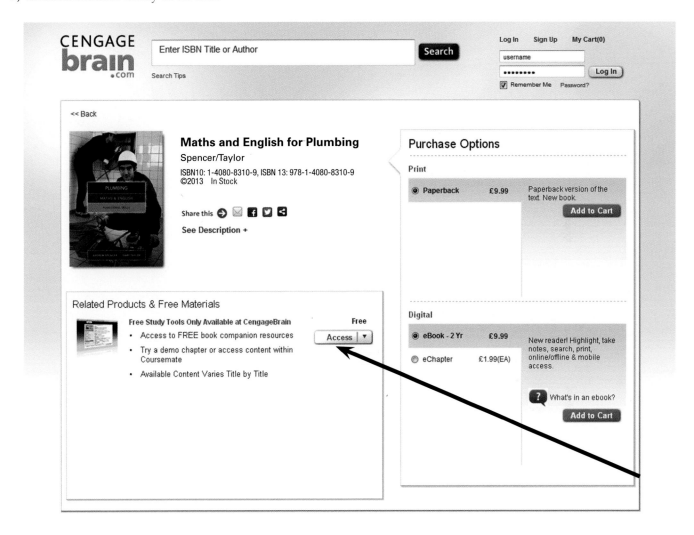

Notes

Notes

Notes

Notes

Notes

Notes

Notes